AF496654

TORQUAY

A HISTORY AND CELEBRATION OF THE TOWN

JOHN BAINBRIDGE

Produced by The Francis Frith Collection
exclusively for

OTTAKAR'S

www.ottakars.co.uk

First published in the United Kingdom in 2005
by The Francis Frith Collection®

Hardback Edition 2005
ISBN 1-84567-755-2

British Library Cataloguing in Publication Data

Torquay - A History and Celebration of the Town
John Bainbridge

The Francis Frith Collection
Frith's Barn, Teffont,
Salisbury, Wiltshire SP3 5QP
Tel: +44 (0) 1722 716 376
Email: info@francisfrith.co.uk
www.francisfrith.co.uk

Printed and bound in England

Front Cover: **TORQUAY, THE STRAND 1920** 69586t

Additional modern photographs by John Bainbridge.

Domesday extract used in timeline by kind permission of
Alecto Historical Editions, www.domesdaybook.org
Aerial photographs reproduced under licence from
Simmons Aerofilms Limited.
Historical Ordnance Survey maps reproduced under licence from
Homecheck.co.uk

Every attempt has been made to contact copyright holders of
illustrative material. We will be happy to give full acknowledgement in
future editions for any items not credited. Any information should be
directed to The Francis Frith Collection.

*The colour-tinting in this book is for illustrative purposes only,
and is not intended to be historically accurate*

Contents

TORQUAY FROM THE AIR 1930 AF33409

Historical Timeline for Torquay

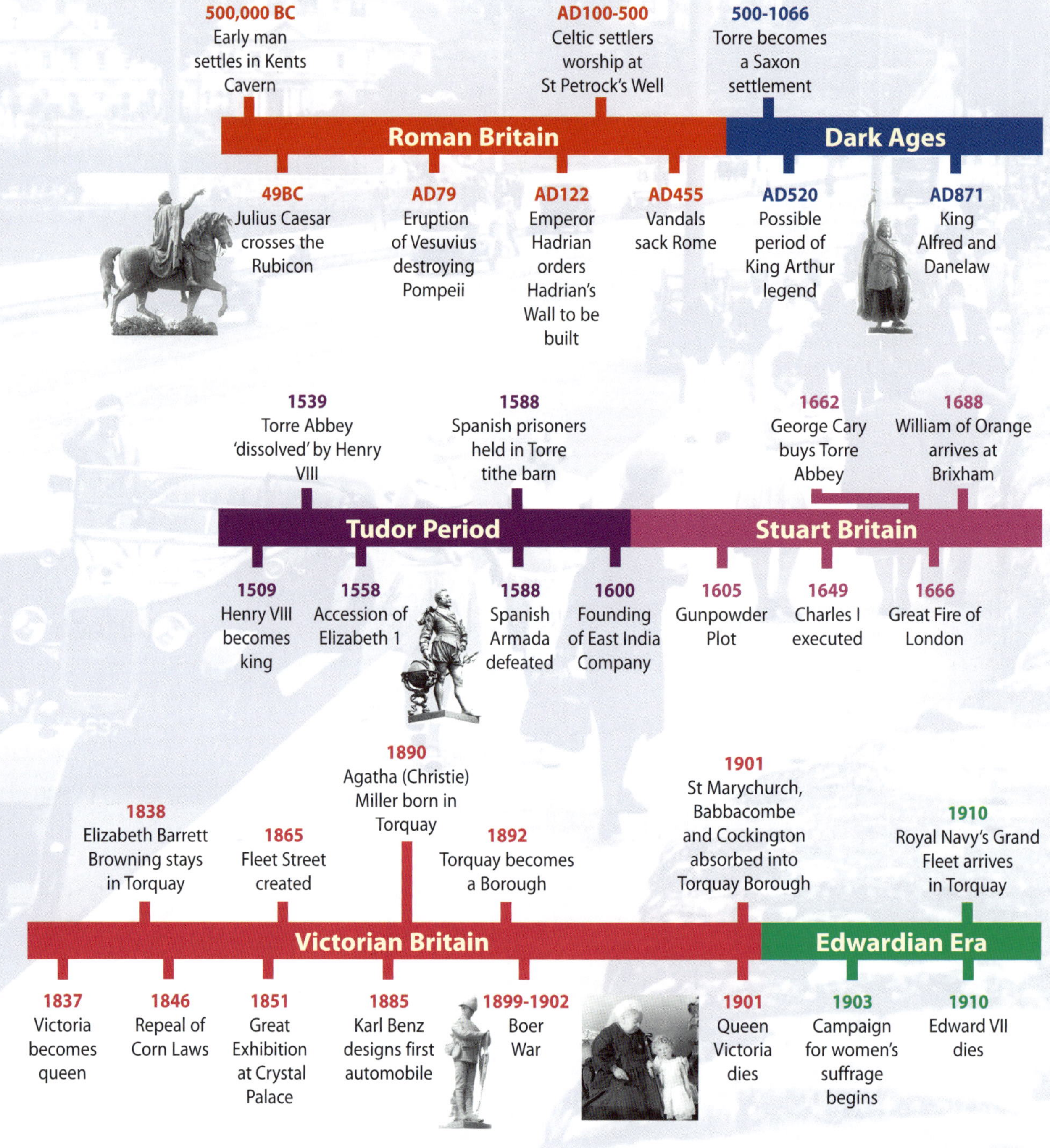

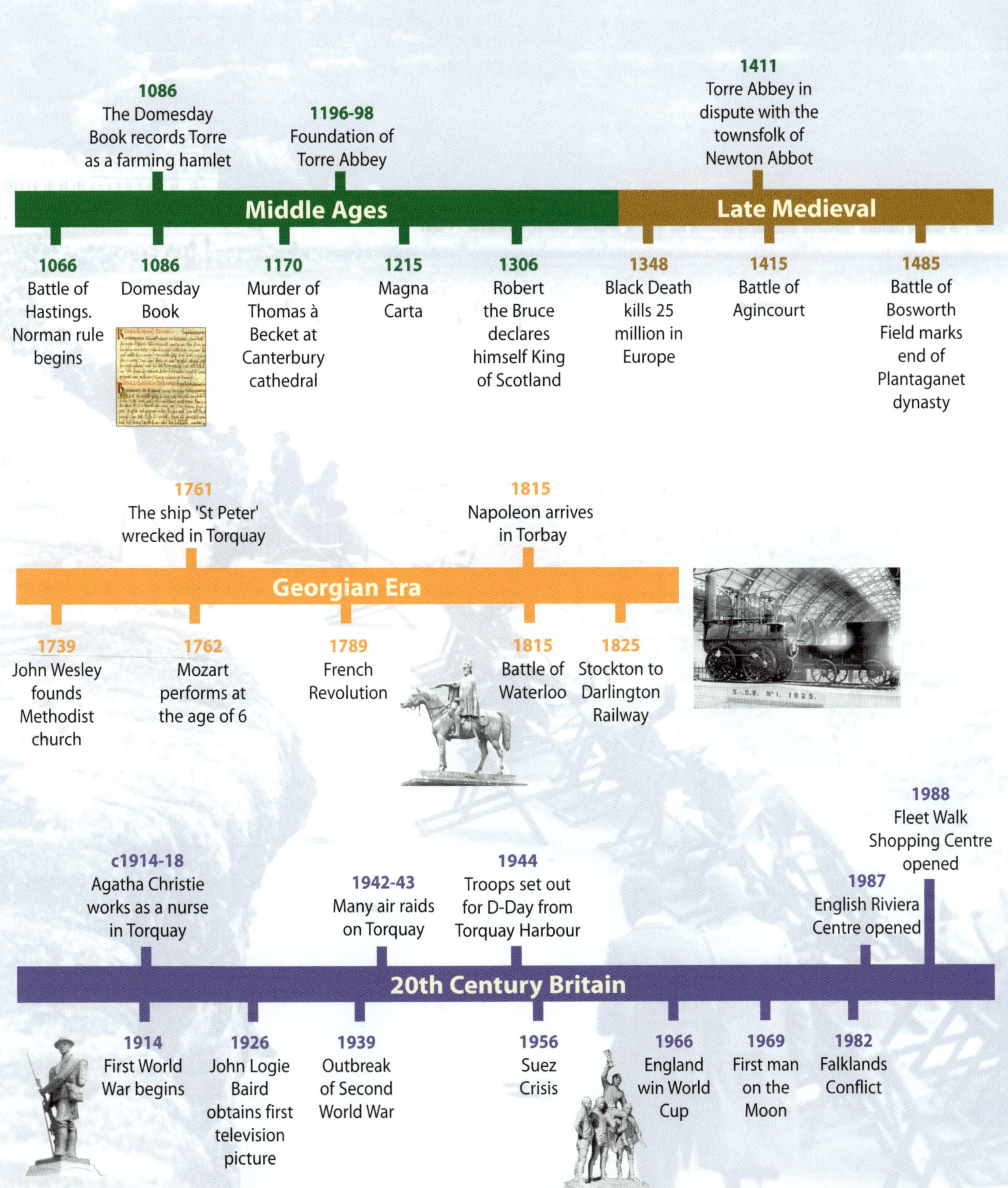

1086
The Domesday Book records Torre as a farming hamlet

1196-98
Foundation of Torre Abbey

1411
Torre Abbey in dispute with the townsfolk of Newton Abbot

Middle Ages

Late Medieval

1066
Battle of Hastings. Norman rule begins

1086
Domesday Book

1170
Murder of Thomas à Becket at Canterbury cathedral

1215
Magna Carta

1306
Robert the Bruce declares himself King of Scotland

1348
Black Death kills 25 million in Europe

1415
Battle of Agincourt

1485
Battle of Bosworth Field marks end of Plantaganet dynasty

1761
The ship 'St Peter' wrecked in Torquay

1815
Napoleon arrives in Torbay

Georgian Era

1739
John Wesley founds Methodist church

1762
Mozart performs at the age of 6

1789
French Revolution

1815
Battle of Waterloo

1825
Stockton to Darlington Railway

S.L.D.R. Nº1. 1925.

1988
Fleet Walk Shopping Centre opened

c1914-18
Agatha Christie works as a nurse in Torquay

1942-43
Many air raids on Torquay

1944
Troops set out for D-Day from Torquay Harbour

1987
English Riviera Centre opened

20th Century Britain

1914
First World War begins

1926
John Logie Baird obtains first television picture

1939
Outbreak of Second World War

1956
Suez Crisis

1966
England win World Cup

1969
First man on the Moon

1982
Falklands Conflict

CHAPTER ONE

A Prehistoric Prelude

TO REGENCY AND VICTORIAN visitors, Torquay was the 'Queen of Watering Places', a well-established resort which was eventually to straddle seven hills, overlooking a huge, half-circular bay. Yet 250 years ago there would have been little to see that resembled the modern layout of the conurbation that now occupies the northern end of Torbay. It is not that Torquay did not have a history before the advent of tourism. The area had a most remarkable past, but a very different one to the last two centuries. Its existence as an early but purpose-built resort has defined its development ever since and tended to overshadow what was there before.

The beauty of Torquay's setting is indisputable. One early visitor compared the town to the best areas of the French Riviera, and today's visitors are greeted by signs welcoming them to the 'English Riviera'. From the first, Torquay's tourists have been captivated by its charms. Napoleon Bonaparte, brought into Torbay after his defeat at the Battle of Waterloo, compared the scene before him to Porto Ferrajo on the island of Elba. Countless thousands since have shared his entrancement and from the resort's beginnings, many of those who came on holiday have settled as residents.

PRINCESS GARDENS AND THE ROCK WALK 1901   47811

Local people have fished the waters of Torbay from the earliest times. One of the grants given by the Norman landlord William Brewer to the monks of Torre Abbey was the right to fish the waters of the bay. Fish were an important part of the religious diet and a number of boats would have set out each day in search of the shoals, though Torquay never became a major fishing port in the way that neighbouring Brixham developed trawling during the Georgian period. The Tudor traveller John Leland did, however, describe Torquay as 'a succour for fishing boats' and the landing stages built for this purpose probably gave Torquay its name. There are few professional fishermen in modern Torquay, though a procession of boats leaves the harbour in the holiday season, full of tourists hoping to make a catch.

FISHERMEN 1888   21445

W G Maton, touring the West Country in the 1790s, remarked, 'Torquay far exceeded our expectations in every respect. Instead of the poor, uncomfortable village that we had imagined, how great was our surprise at seeing such a pretty range of neat, new buildings, fitted up for summer visitors, who may certainly here enjoy convenient bathing, retirement, and a most romantic situation. It commands a full view of Torbay, and is surrounded by a bold amphitheatre of hills, from which the eye may command a prospect of astonishing grandeur and variety.'

But even though these earliest visitors were told stories about the past of this hilly town they probably never guessed quite how exceptional it was. Maton, on his tour, was taken to see the local cave then known as Kents Hole which, he recorded, 'is considered the greatest curiosity in this part of the county'.

KENTS CAVERN ADVERTISEMENT ZZZ03789
(Author's Collection)

KENTS CAVERN 2005 T62716k (John Bainbridge)

An early visit to Kents Cavern was quite an expedition. Two aged women acted as guides, leading Maton's party across the countryside to the mouth of the cave, where they were presented with candles, cleft sticks in which to carry these meagre lights, and a tinderbox. At some points in the exploration Maton and his companions were forced down on to their knees by the low level of some of the passageways, their clothes moistened by the steady drip of water from the roof. Maton wrote afterwards, 'We began to fancy ourselves in the abode of some magician, or (as our companions were two ancient females, and not the most comely of their years) in the clutches of some mischievous old witches, the representation of whose habitations in Shakespeare's Macbeth we could for once persuade ourselves had its foundation in nature.'

Kents Cavern and the history of Torquay are even more remarkable than Maton could have imagined, though the evidence for this was to be gathered very slowly over the succeeding centuries. It is likely that the caves have always been known and a bit of Tudor graffiti from 1571 shows that a William Petre explored the depths, but anything resembling a scientific survey had to wait until the 19th century.

If there was a founding father of archaeological studies in Torquay, then the

> ## *Did you know?*
>
> *A number of people have been lost in Kents Cavern. During the Napoleonic Wars six naval officers entered the cave without a guide. When their candle went out they struggled through the dark passageways for some time, before giving up and collapsing down by a pool of water. Fortunately, they were discovered by local resident William Hyett, who was familiar with the cavern.*

honour should go to John MacEnery, the Roman Catholic chaplain at Torre Abbey. It is not without irony that a churchman was to trigger so much religious controversy, and lead to the modern questioning of the literal truth of the Bible. Inspired by the new craze of cave exploration, the priest had begun excavations in Kents Cavern in 1825, discovering flint implements and the bones of extinct animals together, buried deep

A NATURAL ARCH c1940 T62358

down under layers of mud and stalagmite floor. As the slow growth rate of stalagmites was known, MacEnery, in his report to the British Association, surmised that these remnants of the cave's earliest past must be at least tens of thousands of years old.

The church-dominated scientific establishment of the day exploded with rage at this heresy. Dean Buckland, Professor of Geology at Oxford University, blasted MacEnery's report as being at best unscientific and at worst dangerously irreligious, for in the 17th century, Bishop Ussher had decreed that God had created the world in 4004 BC.

If there were ancient bones and tools under the mud of the cave, Buckland argued, then they had clearly been washed together at the time of Noah's flood and any sort of prehistory before 4004 BC simply didn't come into the equation! This must have been a devastating judgement for poor MacEnery, who looked upon the cave-exploring Professor Buckland as something of a mentor. But he continued to work away by candlelight for a further quarter of a century, though publishing

little else to make such a big impression. Those of MacEnery's finds that did not eventually find their way into Torquay Museum were scattered and lost after his death, a sad epitaph for a man born a little too early in time to receive the scientific credit that was rightly his.

IN KENTS CAVERN 2005 T62710k (John Bainbridge)

**JOHN MacENERY'S GRAVE,
TORRE CHURCHYARD 2005**   T62715k (John Bainbridge)

There is a point in a Kents Cavern tour when the guide switches off the lights, plunging the cave into darkness. It gives an eerie feeling of how it must have felt to be an early cave explorer, with just a fluttering candle to hardly pierce the shadows. This was how William Pengelly encountered the depths of Kents Cavern as he began his investigations into its history. Pengelly was of the new breed of Victorian scientific explorers and, like many prominent Victorians, he was a self-made man. His beginnings were inauspicious; he was born at East Looe in Cornwall in 1812, the son of a sea captain, who initially followed in his father's footsteps and went to sea at the age of 12. This was a very hard life for a child, and even involved being shipwrecked. When his brother died, Pengelly found work ashore so that he might comfort his mother, becoming a pupil-teacher in the local school.

THE VIEW FROM VANE HILL c1877   10399

William Pengelly was a driven man with a real passion for knowledge. Given the time in which he lived and his social background he would have had little chance of admission to a university, but within a few years had acquired a knowledge of mathematics, geology and archaeology that surpassed most 19th-century graduates. As a youth he would walk to Plymouth so that he might have access to a decent library, a round trip on foot of some 30 miles, with the River Tamar to negotiate along the way.

Pengelly came to know Torquay almost by accident, when an acquaintance of his mother related to them both the charms of the growing resort. He resolved to settle there as he saw an opportunity to educate the growing population, opening a private school in Braddon Hill Road. But this was a great cause as well as just a profit-making exercise. Beyond the school's hours, Pengelly made it his mission to educate workers from backgrounds similar to his own. He revitalised the ailing Mechanics' Institute, and began evening classes for those who had no other opportunity to learn. He explored the neighbourhood on foot – for he was a notable pedestrian – recording anything of interest along the way.

Pengelly funded these philanthropic exercises and investigative expeditions by tutoring the children of the better-off; at a time when there were many royal visitors to Torquay he sought out and educated their offspring, one suspects as much for the didactic edification as the money to be earned along the way. One student,

Princess Mary of the Netherlands, later recalled 'the delightful months she had spent in Torquay, and the many geologizing and jollygizing hours for which she was indebted to Mr Pengelly'.

As if this great educational crusade was not enough, Pengelly plunged into a world of research and scientific discovery. In 1844 he had co-founded the Torquay Natural History Society and almost immediately began a geological and archaeological examination of the many local caves, first at Brixham and then Kents Cavern. His popularity as a tutor meant that he was able to give up his school with its restraining hours, and concentrate on this new task in hand.

The Kents Cavern of Pengelly's day was rather different to the show place of today, with its easy access for modern tourists. Many of the tunnels and chambers were filled with mud, hiding the remnants of its ancient history. Some sections were completely impassable. But Pengelly took on the challenge, instigating many of the techniques that are used in archaeological digs to this day, such as a grid system, dividing the floor of the cave into recordable sections. Given the size of Kents Cavern this was a huge undertaking, particularly as much of the work was carried out by flickering candlelight and using the most primitive of hand tools. Pengelly's finds and records of the excavation would eventually fill six volumes of reports, making Pengelly's name a byword for scientific excellence in Victorian England.

It is perhaps fortunate that Pengelly's excavations coincided with the publication

Kents Cavern is Torquay's most visited tourist attraction, having attracted over 6 million visitors since 1880. A hundred years ago the admission price was just 6d. George Smerdon, who worked as a labourer for William Pengelly, excavated at the caves for six days a week. He had a day off for his marriage, but there was little time for a honeymoon as he was back at work in the cave the very next day.

in 1859 of Charles Darwin's book 'The Origin of Species', that revolutionary tome that was finally to see off Bishop Ussher's theory of Creation, proving as it did that life must have existed on Earth for millions of years. Darwin was a visitor to the growing resort of Torquay and corresponded with Pengelly about prehistoric matters. Pengelly's finds, not just from Kents Cavern but also the other caves around Torbay, proved one certainty – that the area was one of the oldest inhabited parts of Britain, and that the Torquay caves must have been occupied for millennia of prehistoric time.

By the time Pengelly died in 1894, this modest, self-educated man had achieved an international reputation. He had co-founded the Torquay Natural History Society, instigated the formation of the Devonshire Association, been elected to membership of the Geological Society and the Royal Society,

Within walking distance of Babbacombe are the wilder landscapes of Petit Tor Down, Daddyhole Plain and Bishop's Walk, all of which give an impression of the wilder rolling landscape that would have been familiar to the occupants of Kents Cavern. Here are the limestone combes, rolling downland and wooded clifftops where Stone Age inhabitants would have hunted game, with the waters of Torbay beyond. Flint arrowheads have been found alongside the paths which now make up the Torquay section of the South West Coastal Footpath. These coastal areas around Torquay have remained relatively unspoiled since this photograph was taken nearly a century ago, still an ideal destination for a ramble or a picnic.

and received the prestigious Lyell Medal for his geological research work. When Pengelly was buried at St Magdalene's Church in Upton, Torquay, his epitaph, composed by himself, had the lines:

His hammer, chisels, compass
lie beside him;
His friends over him piled this
heap of stones.
Alas! Alas! Poor fellow!
Woe betide him
If, in the other world,
there are no bones.

The archaeological investigation of Kents Cavern and other sites around Torquay has continued to this day, and it is comforting to note that John MacEnery's reputation has been vindicated, both by Victorian and modern research, from Pengelly's excavations onwards. For not only has it been proved that man has lived around Torquay for hundreds of thousands of years, but also that Kents Cavern is almost certainly the oldest known habitation in the British Isles. Five flint axes found in the cave date back nearly half a million years, almost certainly knapped into use by Heidelberg Man, who began to settle in Britain in the Lower Palaeolithic Age (Old Stone Age). The cave was occupied by Neanderthal Man and, later, through the ice ages by both man and beast, when the landscape outside would have resembled the arctic tundra of today. Mesolithic hunters sought out game in the cave's rocky neighbourhood. Animals

contemporaneous with human habitation of the district have been found in the dark recesses of Kents Cavern, including cave bears, woolly rhinoceroses, mammoths, sabre-toothed cats, hyenas and lions.

It is interesting to imagine the life of these hunter-gatherer cave dwellers, settling around the fire at the cave mouth - they would rarely have gone deeper into an abyss

Much older than Torquay is the neighbouring village of Cockington, still unspoiled in its deep green valley, though the suburbs of Torquay and Paignton surround it on all sides. A trip to see Cockington Forge, the village's pretty thatched cottages and the stately manor house of Cockington Court is an essential part of any holiday in Torquay. The estate was given by William the Conqueror to William of Falaise for his part in the Norman Conquest, though the manor is Saxon in origin. The Cary family, who were to play a huge part in Torquay's history lived here until 1654, when the estate was sold to the Mallock Family. It was acquired by the Borough Council in 1932 and is now a country park, a residence of badgers, bats, a wide variety of birdlife, and glow-worms.

occupied at various times by wild animals. We know the tools they used, for a great number have been found, washed into the cave's recesses by the deluges of millennia. But we know nothing of their religions or languages. The landscape around what we now know as Torbay has changed considerably, firstly with the disappearance of the land areas that would have once connected England with what is now mainland Europe. For centuries a great forest sprawled across what are now maritime areas off the coast, which was a hunting ground for these early dwellers. But for all Torquay's development since then, it is still possible to get the feel of a more ancient land in the unspoiled green areas of woodland and plain just back from the beaches and clifftops of the modern resort.

COCKINGTON 1901 47821

The Abbey and Manor of Torre

TICKET OFFICE.

TORRE ABBEY GATEHOUSE 2005 T13701k
(John Bainbridge)

THE SMALL band of monks had journeyed a long way from Welbeck Abbey by the time they reached Torbay on, appropriately enough, Lady Day (25 March) in the year 1196. They found a desolate stretch of coastline situated between the older settlements at Paignton and the farming communities of Torre and Ilsham. Though good farmland, it must have seemed wild and deserted compared to the richer agricultural meadows and great forests around their mother abbey in Nottinghamshire. If there were storms during their first weeks at Torre the sea may well have crashed over the beach and onshore, as it often does to this day. Only the religiously devout would have accepted without qualms the challenge of building a great abbey in such a forlorn place.

ABBEY SANDS 1924 76401

At the time of the building of Torre Abbey, the beach ran straight up to the meadows around the religious establishment, offering no shelter from the crashing waves if there was an easterly gale. This stretch of coast remained much the same until Torbay Road and its protecting wall was built during Queen Victoria's reign.

But these canons of the Premonstratensian Order, tried and tested each day by the religious doctrine of St Norbert, whose harsh regime they followed, were used to removing obstacles placed in the way of their faith. Torre Abbey was to be the 23rd house founded by their Order, one of the most respected in Europe – and one of the richest.

The Premonstratensians were Christians on the make, for medieval religious orders were as much about commercial adventure and political influence as sacred devotion and retreat from the world. Premonstratensian canons had worldly functions as well as religious, engaging with the outside world in ways that some other orders did not.

As a community St Marychurch predates Torquay, being a farming settlement in its own right at the time of the Domesday Book, and a Saxon village even before that. It suffered a severe air raid during the Second World War. On 30 May 1943, its church was bombed by a 'tip and run' raider at the time of the Sunday school, tragically killing 23 children and their teachers. It has now been sympathetically restored. St Marychurch has now been absorbed into the larger town of Torquay as a suburb, but has preserved its own identity and is a popular shopping venue. The Irish playwright Sean O'Casey, famed author of 'Juno and the Paycock' and 'The Plough and the Stars', spent the last decades of his life in a house in Trumlands Road, and was a familiar figure as he wandered the streets of Torquay.

Farm workers from the Norman estate of Torre probably watched as the tiny band of canons arrived at the court house. The canons might well have been greeted by the lord of the manor himself, William Brewer, who had donated the land on which the abbey was to be built, along with some farming settlements, the fishing rights in a substantial section of Torbay, and the workers that went with these Norman estates. In charge of the monks was Adam, destined to be the first abbot of Torre and overseer of the building project.

Adam obviously had a talent for the creation of religious houses; within a few years the Order had moved him on to supervise their next foundation. He must have been busy, for the abbey received its charter just two years later, and in the decades that followed the abbey and its monastery expanded into one of the greatest and most profitable religious houses in England, stone for its buildings being brought from as far afield as Portland in Dorset and Beer Quarry in east Devon.

The abbey controlled the life of much of the neighbourhood, including the market at Newton Abbot. It became a centre for learning as books were compiled and schools founded. Hospitals were established so that the sick might be tended, and aid was given to the poor. Its farmland was worked in a far more productive way than it had ever been before, and the fishing rights were exploited as an industry rather than an occasional source of food, leading to the creation of Torquay itself. It is likely that landing stages were built to aid the transportation of stone from distant parts

of the West Country. These were gradually replaced by a larger quay for shipping - 'a succour for fishing boats', according to the Tudor topographer Leland - which gave the new town of Torquay its name, though this may not have appeared until a century or so after the abbey's establishment.

TORRE ABBEY 2005 T13703k (John Bainbridge)

Did you know?

The monks who built Torre Abbey, known as the Premonstratensians, took their name from the Abbey of Premontre in France, which had been founded in the 12th century by St Norbert. By the Middle Ages the Order had over a thousand religious houses scattered around Europe and was one of the wealthiest of religious orders. The monks were known as the White Canons and, despite the harsh Rule of St Norbert which they followed, they engaged very much with the activities of outside society.

The abbey was to be the making of Torre, until then an insignificant hamlet, and lead to the very foundation of Torquay. But to grasp its impact on the landscape, we have to travel back at least 200 years earlier, to the time of the Norman Conquest of Devon. For only then can we understand the status of the abbey's beneficiary William Brewer, and what motivated him to gift much of his personal property to allow it to be built.

Long before there was a place called Torquay there was the hamlet of Torre, some distance inland from the great curve of the bay. In Devon parlance a tor is a rocky outcrop and there are many such in the vicinity of the present resort of Torquay. But the tor that gave a name to the old settlement of Torre is now almost hidden amongst the suburbia east of St Saviour's Church. So concealed is the rock that probably most locals don't know of its existence. Over the centuries the tor has suffered a number of indignities at the hands of man, being a good source of quarried rock. But it survives, and the waters that issue forth would have been venerated in pagan times.

Below the tor is the parish church of St Saviour; but before the Saxons settled hereabouts the dedication was to St Petrock, a Celtic saint, after whom one of the springs that tumbled down from the tor was also named. Pagan beliefs survived alongside early

TOR CHURCH 1889 21473

Once the parish church of St Saviour, this fine building is now the Greek Orthodox Church of St Andrew. This is the original church of Torre, standing on a site that was probably revered in Celtic times. For many years St Saviour's was the only church in the growing town, and was heavily restored in Victorian times. It remains a quiet oasis away from the busy streets of Torre. The churchyard has changed somewhat since this photograph was taken, the gravestones being cleared from some parts and the iron railings removed. Today, a number of white crosses placed alongside the church are in memory of service personnel who died in the Second World War and were buried in far-distant parts of the world.

Christianity and the well of St Petrock may have continued as a source of holy water and a place to leave offerings. It is almost certain that there was a church, albeit a modest chapel, on this site from about the 6th century or 7th century as Christianity spread into Devon. This building may well have been expanded with the arrival of the Saxons, though still modest in size compared to the parish church of today.

TORRE CHURCHYARD 2005   T13702k (John Bainbridge)

A little further inland, on the top of Chapel Hill, is a small chapel dedicated to St Michael, a not uncommon dedication for religious buildings on hilltops for there are several more in Devon, notably at Brent Tor and Brent Hill on the edge of Dartmoor. The area around the tiny chapel is now obscured by trees, but we know that the hill was once bare and visible from the sea. The Reverend John Swete, on his artistic tour of 1793, drew the chapel as being on a barren hillside. It is said that a light was hung here as a signal to mariners out at sea, and well into the 19th century Roman Catholic seamen, harboured in Torquay, would come up to the chapel to pray for a safe passage before continuing their voyages. The chapel was partially repaired a few years ago and is unknown to many locals and visitors.

Whether St Michael's chapel predates the Norman Torre Abbey is unclear, though the date for the present building is 13th-century. It was certainly common to build chapels with that dedication on former pagan sites, with the image of Michael quelling the dragon, so there is a possibility that Torre's early Christians acquired the site for the furtherance of the new religion, the building being erected much later.

In those first years of relative peace after the Norman Conquest, a Norman settler, walking down from the tor to the edge of the sea, at what is now Torquay harbour, would have seen a much wilder landscape than we can probably imagine. Apart from the farming hamlet in the immediate vicinity of the tor and church there would have been little habitation, except a few scattered huts. A small river, the Flete Brook, flowed in fits and starts from its source at Combe Pafford, through woodland towards the sea, along the line of the present Teignmouth and Lymington Roads, then down through marshland near Upton towards what is now the busy junction of Castle Circus. From this point it tumbled down the line of the present day Union Street and Fleet Street – to which it gives its name – to the sea. It must have been an attractive waterway, for the 16th-century topographer John Leland was to wax lyrical about its beauty, 'Here cummith downe a praty Brooke, and renning by the Shore Sandes goith into the Se in Torre Bay.' The Flete Brook remained a feature of the Torquay landscape until the Victorians put it underground in 1865.

The Domesday Book, that great register of Norman acquisitions as they were in 1086, suggests that our Norman settler would have seen what was essentially a farming landscape of fields and sheltering woods, clustered around a dramatic and rocky landscape, rising up from one corner of the great bay.

Domesday also tells us that William the Usher (literally, the usher to the king), now held Torre, having replaced the Saxon Aethelric, and that 'there is land for 7 ploughs. In demesne (land worked for the lord of the manor) are 2 ploughs and 4 slaves; and 16 villans (villagers) and 12 bordars (peasants) with 4 ploughs. There are 24 acres of meadow, and 12 acres of woodland and 200 acres of pasture. Formerly, as now, it is worth 20s'. And worked hard they all would have been, particularly in the early years after the Conquest.

William's invasion of England had not ended at Hastings in 1066, for Devon remained a canker of resistance for a number of years, forcing the Normans to impose the new king's rule in cruel and bloody fashion. Saxon workers in the county probably would have been treated with particular harshness, regarded by the new overlords as being little better than the farm animals they tended.

As conflict fizzled out, however, the new Norman rulers built a more imposing church and an adjacent court manor house, a combination of home and administrative centre for the new lord of the manor. It was to here that Richard de Briwere came to settle when he took over possession from William the Usher in 1088. When King William I

A NORMAN SHIP ZZZ01294

died, the de Briwere's had wisely supported the Conqueror's son William Rufus as heir to the throne. In the subsequent readjustment of land holdings, the family came into favour, acquiring a number of manors including Torre. We know little about this Richard de Briwere (or Brewer as the family came to be called), but his grandson William Brewer was to make a considerable mark on the history of both Torre and the realm of England.

William Brewer, the founder of Torre Abbey, was born in 1150, probably in a dwelling beneath the rocky tor and adjacent to the church, and must have spent his boyhood exploring the fields and woods around the Flete Brook, before seeking preferment at Court. He sailed through the perilous age in which he lived as friend and counsellor to three generations of Angevin kings, including Henry II, Richard the Lionheart, King John and Henry III – a remarkable survival achievement given the Plantagenet family habit of venting their rages on courtiers.

Brewer exercised a number of roles to

ST MARY MAGDALENE CHURCH 1912 64688

The clean lines of St Mary Magdalene engage the eye from many points around Union Street, Upper Union Street and Castle Circus. This church was designed by Anthony Salvin, famous for his restorations of Windsor Castle and the Tower of London, and completed in 1849. Torbay Magistrates Court now occupies the site of the chapel on the far left.

the kings he served; friend, counsellor, politician and cleric. He was a canny lawyer and a considerable statesman – he had to be to survive. Centuries after his death the Tudor topographer Risdon wrote of him as 'a judge and counsellor in Richard's reign, who enjoyed large possessions in that shire (Devon) by the king's gift…he was a man for knowledge, manners, and parentage, right honourable, and highly to be commended'. Brewer may well have been as noble as that, but he had a darker side too, for a contemporary chronicler, the monk Matthew Paris, described the statesman as 'inexorable and cruel'.

Whatever his qualities, Brewer was certainly trusted. While Richard I crusaded in the Holy Land, Brewer was one of the four justices the king left in charge of England. When Richard was captured by Leopold of Austria on his return home, Brewer took charge in the task of raising the considerable ransom demanded for the king's release. He gathered together 70,000 marks towards the 150,000 required, sending this to Austria together with 67 hostages from the English aristocracy as a guarantee that the remainder would be found. The latter must have been a worrying step, for one of the hostages was his son, William Brewer the Younger. Fortunately for the hostages, Leopold of Austria died in 1195, repenting his action, before the further ransom had to be paid and his prisoners were returned home.

Whatever Brewer's temperament he must have been exceedingly pious and grateful for the life of his son, for he made the decision to found and endow a great abbey at Torre in thanks for the safe return of both his son and his king, handing over to its keeping many of his best landholdings in Devon. Within a few years Torre Abbey had become one of the wealthiest religious houses in England.

Brewer was to continue to figure in English history for another quarter of a century, becoming a signatory, though probably a reluctant one, to the Magna Carta in 1215. Nine years later his piety led him to abandon a worldly life, renouncing all of his possessions in favour of his son, William the Younger, in 1224. After taking orders as a monk Brewer died in peaceful old age and was buried at Dunkeswell Abbey in the east of Devon.

His son William the Younger hardly survived him, dying in 1232, though he must have continued to support Torre Abbey during those remaining few years of his life, for he was buried with reverence in the abbey choir. His bones were disturbed in 1770, when debris from the abbey's ruins was taken to fill in the former fish pond. They were found again in 1915 by Colonel Cary, the then owner of the estate, and finally reburied on the site of the abbey choir.

Take away the Victorian buildings and the distant sea wall and this view of Corbyn Sands gives a good impression of what this stretch of coast would have looked like during the time of William Brewer and the canons of Torre Abbey.

Standing today on the parkland of Torre Abbey Meadows, it is hard to imagine the great abbey that once stood here, for little survived Henry VIII's Dissolution of the Monasteries. What does remain shows how magnificent a structure it must have been. John Leland, travelling this way soon after the destruction began, describes 'three fair gate houses', of which only one has survived to the 21st century. The abbey church itself, 168 feet long, is no more, though some of the domestic buildings were converted into a residence for the Ridgeway family in the late 1500s, and there is a magnificent 13th-century tithe barn, one of the oldest surviving buildings in Torquay.

Given the size and wealth of the abbey it is surprising that relatively little is known about the activities of its canons and abbot. One of the few tales relates that local gossips accused Abbot William Morton, appointed in 1382, of beheading Simon Hastings, a canon of the abbey. An inquiry was set up under Bishop Brantlingham to investigate this misdeed, but it transpired that Hastings was demonstrably still alive. The abbot's slanderers were speedily excommunicated. In 1411, the abbey came into conflict with the townsfolk of Newton Abbot, one of its landholdings. The Newtonians, tired of abbey control, had seized control of the local market, turned cattle out on to abbey lands, and – worst of all – appointed their own clergy to take services in the local church. After a lengthy legal wrangle, the nominal victory went to Torre Abbey, but its power began to diminish.

Compared to many abbeys and monasteries, these were minor hiccups in the religious life of England. But when the last abbot, Simon Rede, was appointed in 1523 there seems to have been a feeling that the writing was on the wall, for Rede began to adjust some of the abbey leases as though in anticipation of a dissolution. Torre Abbey was not tainted by the corruption of some religious establishments, nor had it particularly resisted the whims of the king in relation to his divorce from Katherine of Aragon. When the abbey was dissolved in 1539, Rede was allowed to retire to Townstal near Dartmouth with a pension of £64. The abbey's 15 canons were granted pensions of £62 per year. They were fortunate compared to some – Abbot Whiting of Glastonbury Abbey resisted the Dissolution and, for this act of faith or folly, was butchered on the summit of Glastonbury Tor.

Torre Abbey was the wealthiest Premonstratensian foundation in England at the Dissolution, its value being £396 per annum. Its lands and wealth were seized by the Crown, passing through a succession of owners until Sir George Cary bought it in 1662. It remained a Cary family property until 1930, when the remnants of the once great abbey were purchased by Torbay Borough Council. In the years following the Dissolution the abbey crumbled, worn away by the tempestuous gales that sometimes sweep Torbay, its better stone looted for building materials.

The great abbey tithe barn found a use as a place to store the harvest from local farm fields. It was to play one last great part in the history of Torbay. In 1588 the ships of the Spanish Armada struggled their way up the English Channel, beset by the harrying tactics of the smaller English warships, broken from formation by fire vessels, and finally beset by stormy weather.

The Spanish galleon 'Nuestra Senora Del Rosario' had had an unfortunate voyage, colliding with another Spanish ship out in the Channel – an easy prize for Sir Francis Drake who, deserting the battle in favour of this easy plunder, captured her at dawn and had her towed into Torbay. Having removed the Spanish admiral, his officers and various loot, the captured sailors – some 400 in all - were handed over as prisoners into the custody of the county's lord lieutenants Sir George Cary and Sir John Gilbert. These reluctant gaolers, unclear what to do with their 'guests', wrote a despairing letter to London: 'We desire to know your lordships' resolution, what shall become of these people, our vowed enemies. The charge of keeping them is great, the peril greater, and the discontentment over country greatest of all that a nation of so much misliking unto them should remain among them.'

What was left of Torre Abbey belonged to Lord Seymour of Berry Pomeroy and he was given a gift of wine by Cary and Gilbert in exchange for the use of his barn as a temporary gaol. A body of lancers that had been

Following the dissolution of the abbey, Torquay had to wait until the 19th century before new churches were built to cater for the town's growing population. Holy Trinity Church was built in the Gothic style between 1894 and 1896. It has now been converted into a play centre for children.

guarding St Marychurch were brought down to shepherd the Spaniards into the old tithe barn. Cary seems to have been a kindly gaoler for he made each prisoner a cash allowance from his own pocket to enable them to survive, unlike Gilbert who apparently used some of the captives to tend his grounds.

After a couple of weeks 211 of the prisoners were transported to the Exeter Bridewell prison, the rest being allowed to return to their ship. The 'Rosario' was towed round to Dartmouth, before finally being broken up at Chatham. The prisoners were seemingly ransomed and allowed to return to Spain, though tradition alleges that a few settled in Torquay, fathering dark-haired children, the descendants of whom might be seen to this day. Since that time the old Torre Abbey barn has been known as the Spanish Barn.

The value of Torbay as a shelter for shipping, against the Channel storms, was probably recognised quite early on. There are anecdotal tales of Viking longships hiding in the bay, though there was little plunder to be had there – unlike the neighbouring villages of Teignmouth and Exmouth, which were raided. There is a possibility that the Saxon leader Ceorl defeated, with very great slaughter, a Danish army at Weekaborough, a little way inland, though the location of this battle is much disputed.

THE SPANISH BARN 2005 T62707k (John Bainbridge)

A TUDOR SHIP ZZZ01290

In the years following the intrusion of the Spanish Armada, Torbay seemed very much to be an 'open' anchorage, used by any passing foreign privateer, pirate and hostile man of war. This cavalier treatment of national boundaries caused much dismay with the local magistrates and deputies, charged with the defence of the realm and keeping the peace. In June 1635, a dozen Dutch warships anchored in the bay, an act of war in fact, though the locals chose not to provoke hostility by seeking a confrontation. An increased number of English fighting ships patrolling the Channel, during and immediately after the English Civil War, proved a deterrent to most of these abuses. But there were still incidents.

In 1667 the Dutchman Admiral de Ruyter, frustrated at failing to intercept an English convoy loaded with goods from the Levant, sailed with his fleet into Torbay. The Dutchman must have felt particularly confident, having already defeated the British navy off Dunkirk the previous year, and managing to destroy a good portion of the home fleet in the Medway days earlier. The Dutchman set fire to two English vessels off Torquay and fired his cannon at Torre Abbey, but was not equipped to make a more substantial landing. He stayed in the bay, sailing up and down the Devon coast with little resistance, for a few weeks before heading back out to sea.

That expedition might well have inspired Captain Roche of the French Navy to put into Torbay on a cold February day in 1668. No one resisted as the Frenchman landed a considerable number of armed men and marched towards Torquay harbour in search of loot. The ship 'Mary', of Ostend, then a port in the Spanish Netherlands, had crept into the harbour a little while earlier, seeking escape from the perils of the English Channel. The 'Mary's' captain and crew had scuttled their vessel and handed over cargo and guns to Daniel Luscombe, a local citizen in Torquay. Despite the fact that the 'Mary' was half underwater she still represented considerable plunder to Roche, who had her caulked, refloated and taken out to sea.

But Roche went much further than that, demanding – possibly at gunpoint – the cargo and guns in the possession of Daniel Luscombe. Roche got what he wanted, sailing out of Torbay with both ship and goods. As England and France were at peace at the time and their two kings amenable to each other this was an extraordinary act of piracy. Not that Roche benefited very much. Two weeks later his little convoy was intercepted by Sir Thomas Allin of the English Navy, who forced him to hand over his booty and leave English waters for good.

Soon after Roche's adventure, there is one of the first recorded instances of the bay off Torquay being used for pleasure yachting. In 1671, King Charles II and his brother, James, Duke of York, took a leisurely cruise up and down the Channel, anchoring for a while off Torquay. There were a number of yachts and accompanying warships in the party, and the locals no doubt lined the waterfront to catch a rare glimpse of this colourful monarch.

It was a peaceful interlude in history's more martial use of Torbay. Scarcely 20 years later William of Orange sat on the throne, and England found itself in conflict with the French and the deposed English monarch James II – the James of that leisurely cruise in 1671. William had landed with a massive army at Brixham in 1688, marching to London to take the throne both in his name and that of Queen Mary, his wife and James's daughter, and to uphold the constitutional rights of Parliament and Protestant England. The exiled James had sought friends at the French court, and there were considerable fears of a French assault on southern England.

Whilst William sought out James's army in Ireland, the French warrior Admiral de Tourville set out from the naval port at Brest, to defeat the English fleet off Beachy Head in Sussex. Encouraged by this victory he headed down the Channel and anchored in Torbay. De Tourville had hoped to find

sympathisers for James as he travelled along the coast, but met only opposition. British troops lined Torbay, waiting to challenge him, so he set out for home – though not before destroying by fire the neighbouring town of Teignmouth. The next day King William defeated James's army at the Battle of the Boyne and secured his throne.

It was just after this time that Daniel Defoe, the author of 'Moll Flanders' and 'Robinson Crusoe', visited the area during one of his many peregrinations around Britain. Like many others he recognised that the bay was one of England's few great natural anchorages: 'Torbay, of which I know nothing proper to my observation, more than it is a very good road for ships, though sometimes, especially with a southerly or south-easterly wind, ships have been obliged to quit the bay and put out to sea, or run into Dartmouth for shelter.'

This vulnerability to certain winds could wreck ships in the bay, though this might often be to the profit of Torquay people. In 1761 the brig 'St Peter' was driven into Torbay by an easterly gale, crashing ashore just west of Torre Abbey. The crew managed to scramble up on to land, but £4,000 worth of cargo was seized by local plunderers who even mugged the ship's captain for his watch. It was one of the few recorded instances of shipwreck in Torbay – there were many more unreported.

In the mid 18th century a series of deafening explosions rang out, echoing around the valleys and cliffs of the growing town of Torquay and frightening the sea birds over the bay. Anxious locals who were not in the know may have looked out into the Channel for the cause of these disturbances, but this particular destruction was domestic in origin. Mr George Cary, the local landowner, was blowing up the great church of Torre Abbey.

His ancestor Sir George Cary had acquired Torre Abbey in 1662, building a mansion on the site of the old refectory. His descendants added to the building over the next two centuries, laying out the parkland. They had utilised some of the abbey buildings, but the 168 feet long church was too great a proposition to incorporate. Some of the stones had been removed for other uses in the years after the Dissolution, with Torbay's storms adding to the sense of neglect and decay.

This is the Torquay that William Pengelly would have known, a town at the height of its Victorian splendour, still centred over seven hills. Just right of the centre, Fleet Street – just over two decades in existence - runs through the heart of the town to the harbour and St John's Church dominates the hillside on the right of the picture. Notice how narrow Torbay Road is as it runs between Vane Hill and the sea. The Princess Gardens and pier did not exist in 1888. Thousands of tons of earth were dumped into the sea here to create an extension to the land mass, creating the gardens we know today.

THE FLEET IN TORBAY 1904   52950a

Ships of the Royal Navy have continued to use Torbay as an anchorage up to recent times, an echo of the days of the Spanish Armada and the wars with the Dutch and the French. This photograph shows a gathering of the fleet in Edward VII's reign. Perhaps the last great occasion when so many ships gathered here was during the Review by Queen Elizabeth II to mark her Silver Jubilee in 1977.

By the 18th century, the abbey that was once Abbot Adam's great creation was in a parlous state, the ruins dangerous to walk amongst; hence George Cary's dramatic 'clearing up'. But something of Adam's religion survived all of this destruction and dissolution, for the Cary family were staunch Roman Catholics, worshipping in secret when they had to, and openly after the Relief Act of 1778 freed them from that restriction. The year after that liberating Act of Parliament, they built a church in what had been the monastic guest hall, which remained the only Roman Catholic place of worship in Torquay until 1854. It was here that John MacEnery officiated in his role as chaplain; that is, when he was not excavating Kents Cavern. There is a kind of roundness therefore, leading from the development of Torre Abbey way back to Torquay's prehistoric history.

And what of Torre itself, around the turn of the 19th century? Its days as a manorial farming settlement were over, and the glory of Torre Abbey a moment of the past. Torre, once the heart of this community, was becoming bypassed by the development of a town nearer to the little Flete Brook, with houses and a little port clustered around the harbour that the Abbey's canons had created. From the late 1700s onwards, the history of Torre was to become absorbed in the greater story of Torquay.

New housing around Waldon Hill made a new church necessary as a convenience for new residents. St Luke's, with its unusual design, became renowned for its view over Torre Abbey Sands, and a prominent landmark when seen from out at sea.

Did you know?

The Mohun family from Dunster came into the possession of the Manor of Torre in the 14th century. The remaining gateway of Torre Abbey is sometimes called the Mohun Gate, probably in honour of Sir John de Mohun who may have paid for its construction. Torre is sometimes called Tormuhun after the family.

The Queen of Watering Places

ON A JULY DAY in 1815, the 74-gun ship HMS 'Bellerophon' – known affectionately to its crew as 'Billy Ruffian' - dropped anchor in Torbay, after a brief voyage from France. Its captain, Frederick Maitland, was on the most important command of his career, his passenger being the recent Emperor of the French, Napoleon Bonaparte.

'Bellerophon' had been in the process of being broken up when Napoleon escaped from exile on the island of Elba, landing in France to seize power in the brief 100 days of glory leading up to his final defeat at Waterloo. In this emergency, the ship was hurriedly re-commissioned to form part of a fleet guarding the English Channel. After attempts to escape to America, Napoleon agreed to seek a passage on the ship to England, so that he might – astonishingly – seek sanctuary in the country that he had fought for so many years. Maitland treated Napoleon with considerable respect, giving

the emperor the impression that he was more passenger than prisoner. Napoleon certainly seems to have been deluded into believing that he was a guest. The truth is that the British government had not the slightest intention of again letting their old enemy escape to cause yet more mayhem on the Continent.

Napoleon's arrival off Torquay was a sensation. Here was the 'monster' whose very name had been used to frighten children

to sleep, a warrior whose activities had cost tens of thousands of British lives both at sea and on battlefields across Europe, and who had threatened to invade these very shores on several occasions. Here he was, Napoleon Bonaparte, sometime Emperor of France, almost within hailing distance of Torquay's beaches. But instead of fear and animosity, Torquay treated Napoleon as a hero and his visit became a spectacle, the like of which Torquay had never seen before.

The Emperor had entranced the ship's company of 'Bellerophon' on the voyage across the Channel. Captain Maitland later recalled that Napoleon's manners were 'extremely pleasing and affable, he joined in every conversation, relating numerous anecdotes, and endeavoured in every way to promote good humour'. He laughed and joked with the crew, gave Maitland a friendly pat on the head, and even attended theatricals laid on by the ship's junior officers. Napoleon gave the embryonic Torbay tourist industry one of its earliest commendations - *'enfin, voila un beau pays!'* ['at last, here is a beautiful country!') before, famously, comparing its shores to Porto Ferrajo on the island of Elba. These comments were much quoted at the time and have been ever since, for Torquay had never welcomed a more famous visitor, or one who drew such a large crowd of visitors quite so quickly.

A local man recorded the spectacle: 'There never were before or since such an assembly of craft in Torbay. Torquay was little more than a fisherman's village, but the population, such as it was, seemed to have turned out altogether…all the country seemed to come in. Gentlemen and ladies on horseback and in carriages; other people in carts and wagons; and to judge by the number of people, all the world inland was flocking to see Bonaparte … it seemed a gala day as the boats thronged around 'Bellerophon.'

Ashore in Torquay, the ship's officers were approached by young ladies, full of questions about the 'Bellerophon's' unusual passenger. Midshipman Home of the 'Bellerophon' – who had been captivated by Napoleon on the journey from France - clearly enjoyed this popularity, telling the ladies of Torquay that if they but met the Emperor they would fall madly in love with him.

Though beneficial for the economy of Torquay - and some of the boatmen were said to have earned a month's income in two days - the situation was now becoming embarrassing for officialdom. Hundreds of little boats clustered around the 'Bellerophon', their passengers enthusiastically chanting 'Boney! Boney!' and rewarding every glimpse of Napoleon with great cheers. Napoleon seems to have relished this unexpected popularity, making frequent appearances on the ship's decks and at the stern windows - all the better to be seen. It was not the reaction the British government wanted towards its vanquished enemy, and at some point during the brief two days that the 'Bellerophon' laid at anchor in Torbay Napoleon learned that he was not to be welcomed ashore.

It is likely that Napoleon garnered this bad news from hostile leaders in newspapers taken aboard ship. He had hoped to enjoy the support of the Prince Regent in seeking an exile in England, sending a letter to the Prince that he 'came like Themistocles to throw himself upon the hospitality of the British people – I put myself under the protection of their laws, which I claim from Your Royal Highness, as the most powerful, the most constant, and the most generous of my enemies'. His initial treatment aboard the 'Bellerophon' and the reception in Torbay must have deluded him into thinking that he had been granted his wish. It was not to be. After 48 hours, the 'Bellerophon' set sail for Plymouth where guard boats kept the curious public at bay. Soon afterwards Napoleon Bonaparte was on his way to exile and eventual death on the Atlantic island of St Helena.

The people of Torquay were probably right to take Napoleon so much to their hearts, for his activities in Europe did much to create the very concept of the fashionable seaside resort. The local observer of Napoleon's visit might well have described Torquay as 'little more than a fishermen's village', but it was already a settlement where fishing, boatbuilding and other nautical activities had to share the coastline with pleasure and leisure pursuits and, above all, as a remedy for poor health.

From the earliest times, Torbay had been a natural haven for shipping. The constant wars with France in the 18th century had led to it being an important anchorage for the Royal Navy, usefully within striking distance of the French coast, and as a refreshing post for ships blockading French ports. The little quay established by the canons of Torre Abbey was expanded to allow munition boats to load supplies for the great fleet of warships out in Torbay.

During the early years of Napoleon's reign there were very real fears of a French invasion of England, with steps being taken to evacuate the population if an attempt was made. There was even a suspicion that Torbay was to be Napoleon's chosen landing ground. A town meeting considered the removal of women and children which decreed that 'the infirm and children under eight, who were incapable of walking 10 miles a day should, in case of alarm, be assembled in three divisions at a specified rendezvous and, be removed to Dartmoor in carts'. As a deterrent and to protect the shipping in the bay a great fort was built on Berry Head, with cannon pointing both out to sea and inland. Troops were quartered at several points around Torbay to fend off any French infantry that had the temerity to land.

THE NATURAL HISTORY MUSEUM 2005 T62719k (John Bainbridge)

Officers stationed in Torquay or on the naval vessels based in Torbay would send for their wives and families to join them and new villa residences and more substantial cottages were built. With the state of war, the wealthy were barred from touring the Continent, bringing a host of sightseers to the southern coasts of England. But if war was the starting point of Torquay's development as a seaside resort, then it was the care of invalids that kept the town alive after the conclusion of the Napoleonic Wars. It may well have been that medical men attached to the fleet first noticed the potential of Torquay as a health resort. Interestingly, Croydon's 'Guide to the Watering Places of South Devon', published just two years after Napoleon's visit, makes no mention of any naval influence on the growth of the resort, only saying that it was built 'to accommodate invalids'.

In 1832 Mr Octavian Blewitt, guidebook author of 'A Panorama of Torquay', walked across its hills and regarded a town that was already far more than a fishing village. Acknowledging the importance of the naval presence at the start of his century he says that this was just the beginning: 'When, therefore, subsequent observations had confirmed the testimony of public opinion in (Torquay's) favour, houses were erected for the accommodation of the invalids, who annually migrate from the colder parts of the Island to Devonshire'. But Blewitt had a concern that the rapid expansion of the town would cause the very health problems people came to Torquay to escape: 'The nearer the place approximates to the character of a town the more serious will be the injury to that climate which is now the source of its prosperity.'

What did the rapidly expanding town of Torquay look like to Blewitt? The best description we have comes from a guidebook published just four years earlier: 'The rise of the salubrious winter resort and delightful summer watering place of Torquay had been singularly rapid, it containing about 130 genteel and commodious houses, either occupied by resident gentry, or used as lodging houses; and at the Royal Hotel, if any man had the silver, he might live as well as in any part of England'. But not everyone thought Torquay improved by this expansion. The writer Walter Savage Landor mourned the older Torquay, writing that since he first saw Torquay 40 years previously 'six or seven thatched cottages had been replaced by smart, ugly houses and rich, hot-looking people. It was still the most beautiful watering place in the British dominions, but deprived of its ancient refinement'.

There were baths in the new resort of Torquay as early as 1817, for a guidebook tells us of 'the commodious warm and cold sea water baths built by Mr Pollard at the extremity of the pier'. The poet Elizabeth Barrett Browning took advantage of these baths, afterwards part of the Regent Hotel, on her stay in Torquay in 1838. The value of water as a cure-all was at the height of its popularity. Customers could be subjected to a variety of treatments such as bathing in salt water, fresh water, hot or cold water, with the added option of taking all of the above internally.

ODDICOMBE BEACH 1889 21491

These bathing machines would allow customers, mostly ladies, to enter on shore so that they might change into the ponderous swimming costumes of the day. The machine would then be taken into the sea so that the lady might enter the water and be seen as little as possible by passing males.

In its dramatic position immediately above the sea, the Imperial Hotel dominates the northern edge of the town. Westley's 1882 'Tourist Guide to Torquay' says that it was the most frequented hotel in the town and that 'this splendid edifice…embraces all the modern appliances found in these new hotels which as commercial speculations have been so successful at other watering places and the Metropolis. Here the courteous manager, Mr Hussey, has had the honour of receiving Her Majesty

THE IMPERIAL HOTEL 1888 21436

the late Queen of Holland, the late Emperor of the French, and HRH the Prince of Wales (who finds the steps to the water very convenient for the landing from his yacht).' At the time of writing the Imperial Hotel was about to begin a further massive modernisation.

Sea bathing had acquired a considerable reputation following King George III's exploits along the coast at Weymouth, where His Majesty would plunge into the Channel to the accompaniment of a brass band playing the National Anthem. Torquay was not far behind in this respect, though it had not yet enjoyed much in the way of royal patronage. Nonetheless, the beaches were superb, the sands at Abbey Sands being some eight feet deep. Men would bathe at such places, taking dips – often naked – into the briny waters of Torbay. In these early times, women were confined to the coves below Beacon Hill, where a couple of bathing machines might be hired to convey overdressed ladies into the sea in the most modest way possible. Mixed bathing was absolutely forbidden in Torquay until 1899. The town's Board of Health ruled that 'no person of the male sex shall at any time bathe within 50 yards of a ladies bathing machine'. Bathing 'with or without the wearing of drawers' was frowned upon along the seashore between the Belgrave and Imperial Hotels.

We tend to think of seaside holidays as brief summer occasions, but early visitors, particularly those who had come to Torquay in search of better health, would stay for prolonged periods of time and at all seasons of the year. Indeed, the initial fame of Torquay was as a winter, not a summer resort. Hardier souls would take to the waters of the bay as readily in December as August. These first visitors to Torquay had a choice of lodgings. Octavian Blewitt observed 'the invalid will find in Torquay a variety of excellent

THE LADIES' BATHING COVE c1890 T62801

accommodation in the way of houses; those of the higher class are equal in comfort to any on the coast … small houses for the reception of limited families are to be obtained in different parts of the place. The cottage villas with gardens and shrubberies on the hills are frequently preferred by those who prefer a detached residence.'

The biggest killer of the Victorian age was consumption, or tuberculosis as we call it today. The rich for all their advantages were not immune to this dreadful disease, which spread out from the poverty of the overcrowded slums and rookeries that often backed on to their town houses, or which might be encountered in many a run-down country cottage, for rural poverty too plumbed to new depths in the years following the Napoleonic Wars. It was the disease whose very name could be denied. The wealthy patrons of Torquay were seldom described as 'consumptive': more usually they were people with 'delicate lungs' or more simply - as in Mr Blewitt's guide - 'invalids'. John Murray's

Did you know?

In 1866 a cyclone roared into Torbay, severely damaging the sea front, sinking 50 ships at anchor off Torquay and killing 100 people. The fishermen of neighbouring Brixham very bravely put to sea in their trawlers and saved a great many lives. The disaster made national headlines, as have the many storms that have hit Torquay since.

'Handbook for Devon and Cornwall' (1854) extolled the benefits of seeking the 'cure' at Torquay, giving us a good description of the town at that time: 'The general effect of the white houses, the gray limestone cliffs, and the foliage and greensward forming the ground of the whole, is unusually pleasant and picturesque, and calculated to soothe, as far as scenery can soothe, the lassitude and

depression of ill-health.' Murray's handbook tells us that Torquay was 'much resorted to by invalids with delicate lungs'.

Doctor Radclyffe Hall, who made a good living from tending consumptives in Torquay, was very positive about the effects of a break in the town: 'When a consumptive invalid … has been in Torquay for only two or three days, he usually finds his breathing is easier, his restlessness less and his skin softer and cooler in the evening.'

Visitors making a briefer stay in Torquay would put up at one of the several hotels that had sprung up in the vicinity of the harbour. The Royal Hotel (or more properly Poulton's Royal Hotel), which had started out as the modest London Inn, was extended in 1821 at the junction of Torwood Street with the

Strand, offering exceptional views over a similarly enlarged Torquay Harbour. The Royal boasted the nearest ballroom to the sea, designed by the renowned architect John Foulston. It was here that the future Queen Victoria stayed in 1833, having stepped ashore from the yacht 'Emerald' on to that part of the harbour now called Victoria Parade in her honour. Nearby were Torquay's other two hotels; the Family Hotel (afterwards the Queen's Hotel) and Cole's Commercial Inn - patronised, as the name suggests, by those who came into the resort on business.

By the time of Victoria's visit, three stagecoaches arrived in the town every day, bringing mail and passengers, with private carriages probably bringing a great many more visitors. It was still not unusual for some visitors to arrive - as Princess Victoria had - by sea, for despite the growth of the town the road network that we know today was nowhere near complete.

As recently as 1793 the Reverend John Swete, touring the district, had described one Torbay lane, probably typically, as having 'more the appearance of the deserted channel

A COACHING PRINT ZZZ01291

THE ROCK WALK 1904 52949

of a torrent than the way leading to a town'. Many of the lanes around Torquay probably served local farmsteads in Saxon times. During the heyday of Torre Abbey these byways were almost certainly kept in good order by the church as essential thoroughfares for abbey traffic, but with the dissolution of the abbey many fell into disrepair. Even the best could hardly cope with the demands of a growing resort. Not that the journey into Torquay was unattractive. Octavian Blewitt commented that it was 'the most beautiful line of road in the county, and constitutes one of the leading attractions on the way of excursions from Torquay'.

At some time in 1814 the local baronet Sir Lawrence Vaughan Palk, commonly known as Sir L V Palk and lord of the manor of Torwood, took a walk near Chapel Hill. His father had died the previous year and the family finances were in some disarray. Palk was just 20 years old, a minor in the eyes of the law, though - by the standards of the time - a benevolent character and notably courageous. In 1821, he dived into Torquay harbour to save a child from drowning, and a few years later opened a Mechanics' Institute in the town, to further

UPPER UNION STREET 2005   T62704k (John Bainbridge)

the education of working men. His family had invested considerable sums both in the development of the resort and the harbour, with scant return. A friend who walked with him suggested that Torquay was suffering because of the poor quality of the local roads, which made access difficult for the kind of clientele the town needed to attract.

Palk pondered this dilemma as he walked amongst the woodlands around St Michael's chapel, then realised the solution lay in the very course of his ramble. In the days that followed he worked his way through the wood with his woodsman George Pearce, marking out the line of a new road into the top of Torquay, the better to connect the resort with the neighbouring market town of Newton Abbot - one of the main access points in the county. Those motorists who now speed along the route between Newton Abbot and Torquay are following in Palk's footsteps.

By 1826, a turnpike trust had been established to build new roads in the vicinity, for which a charge was made for use. These newer thoroughfares are very much the roads that we follow around Torquay today. With the opening of a bridge across the Teign estuary in 1827, a road was built into Torquay from that direction. As this came into the expanding town from the direction of Maidencombe, it followed the line of the Flete Brook from the direction of Combe Pafford, meeting Palk's route to Newton Abbot and then down into what is now Union Street. Lower and Upper Union Street were built at much the same time, the latter through the nursery gardens of the Morgan family. The Flete Brook somehow managed to survive these highways along its banks, though it was sunk into a culvert in the vicinity of Union Street. These new roads led to the building of a number of houses at the top end of Torquay.

Around where Fleet Street now meets Union Street was the turnpike gate, where carriages and horses would halt to pay a fee so that they might use the turnpike road. (A local worthy, Mr Templer of Stover near Newton Abbot, famously got his horse to jump the turnpike gate on Shaldon Bridge to avoid paying!) The turnpike into Torquay was a profitable exercise for its trust, raising nearly £4,000 in 1840 alone.

Given that only pedestrians were free of the toll, the gate was hugely unpopular with anyone who drove a carriage or rode a horse. Locals muttered 'obnoxious gate!' to each other as they approached and had to pay this levy on their free movement, and by 1842 the townsfolk were already petitioning for its removal. They were helped by the rapid expansion of Torquay, for common law dictated that no turnpike gate could be placed within a mile of a town and that, anyway, the gate was only supposed to be in place until the roadbuilding debts had been paid off - and that had been achieved years before. The Turnpike Trustees, most of whom, after all, had to live in the town, agreed and in 1849 the gate was removed. New turnpike gates were built further out on the Newton Abbot, Teignmouth and St Marychurch roads.

ST JOHN'S CHURCH 1904   52952

St John's Church dominates the view from all around Torquay's harbour. It was designed by the great Victorian architect George Edmund Street to replace an earlier chapel which stood on the same site. The church was completed in 1871, the top of the tower being added by Street's son in 1883. Much of the building was constructed from limestone quarried from the nearby hillside.

Travel from Torquay to the neighbouring resort of Paignton remained problematic until the 1840s, a winding and difficult road going from one to the other via Livermead. Everyone knew that the natural route between the two towns lay along the sea front, across the point where the extensive grounds of Torre Abbey rolled down to the sea, but there remained a formidable obstacle in the shape of Mr H G Cary, the abbey's owner. In 1836, an approach was made to Mr Cary requesting that he might allow such a construction, but Cary argued vociferously against a road that would, in his words, 'pass within 200 yards of my dining room'.

Besides, Cary argued, this was potential building land and would have to be paid for at commercial building land rates. This was probably a bluff for it is unlikely that Cary would ever have wanted the sea view from his home interrupted by any development at all. He told the turnpike trustees that he would have no objection to a circuitous route around the back of Torre Abbey if that would suit, but this was unacceptable to the townsfolk who wanted the road to provide better access to Abbey Sands.

A more reasonable objection put forward by the stubborn Mr Cary was that a route along the edge of the sea would be vulnerable to easterly gales - and this has certainly proved to be true, as anyone who has witnessed the waves crashing over the present highway can testify. A Victorian observer noted that 'it is defended by a broad sea wall, or rather, we should say, appears to be defended; for the heavy swell which rolls into the bay during

TORBAY ROAD 1928 81116

south east gales has more than made sad havoc with the opposing rampart, and played with its massive blocks as a child does with its marbles'.

But in 1840 the Torquay Turnpike Act was renewed by Parliament for a further 30 years and work began. This beautiful but troubled stretch of road took two years to lay down and cost £13,000. But, even as the first travellers wended their way above Torre Abbey Sands, it continued to be controversial. A turnpike gate was established close to the present day Rock Walk, inconveniencing those who wished to travel even a modest distance alongside the sea, and which was eventually to catch out anyone taking a vehicle to and from Torquay railway station. There were great cheers when, in 1859, a storm washed it away. A stouter building put in its place faced the eventual ignominious fate of being converted into a sea front public convenience. The thoroughfare so dreaded by Mr Cary was first called, rather unimaginatively, New Road, then Station Road, before gaining the name we know it by today - Torbay Road.

ABBEY CRESCENT 1896 38598

ABBEY CRESCENT 2005 T62702k (John Bainbridge)

The opening of Torquay railway station in 1859 led to the speculative development of dwellings in what had previously been a quiet area of town. Abbey Crescent was completed in 1858. For much of the 20th century the western half of the Crescent was familiar to locals and visitors as the Palm Court Hotel. Photograph T62702k, taken in 2005, shows how this once beautiful crescent of houses has declined in recent years.

The railway first came to Torquay from neighbouring Newton Abbot in 1848. Originally, there were plans to route the track down the line of the present-day Union Street and Fleet Street to the harbour. The great engineer Isambard Kingdom Brunel intended the line to be part of his 'atmospheric railway' experiment, where a series of steam pumps extracted the air from a pipe set between the railway lines, with the resulting vacuum pulling the trains along, but this was abandoned in favour of the more traditional steam train. The railway station at Torre was opened on 15 December 1848, and the Torquay Station, in Cockington parish, on 11 July 1859. Both stations were some distance from the heart of the new resort, nonetheless this was the way most visitors arrived in Torquay for over 100 years.

Leland's pretty Flete Brook was not to survive much longer in the face of these new road developments. As early as 1793, the Reverend John Swete had visualised how this approach to Torquay might change: 'Instead of the meadow being frittered away by an insignificant row of houses that skirt the brook and block its exit to the sea, it might have been converted into a handsome street which would have opened to the water and formed an approach to it of unparalleled beauty.'

In 1865 Swete's vision came true, though without the help of the Turnpike Trust. It was the Local Board of Health that decided to improve what was a very run down area of shops and cottages by a combination of demolition and road building. The Flete Brook, so familiar to Saxon farmers, Norman overlords, medieval monks and Georgian travellers, finally disappeared into a tunnel - soon to become a major sewer - as the new road, called Fleet Street in the brook's honour, finally appeared. In the last decades of Victoria's reign the residents and visitors of Torquay became familiar with the main streets of the town as we know them today, and could take the long journey down Upper Union Street, Union Street and Fleet Street to Torquay harbour.

FLEET STREET 1906 54027

FLEET STREET 2005 T62703k (John Bainbridge)

THE OLD TOWN HALL 2005   T62706k (John Bainbridge)

THE NEW TOWN HALL 2005 T62718k (John Bainbridge)

Photograph T62706k (left) shows Torquay's original Town Hall, a modest building completed in 1851 on the junction of Union Street and Abbey Road. The more imposing current Town Hall and Borough Council Offices (above) were completed in 1912, incorporating a grand hall for fairs and performances and the public library. A new road access from the direction of Teignmouth, Lymington Road, led to the creation of a new road junction - Castle Circus.

Market Street was created, sloping downwards to a junction at Union Street in 1853. Torquay had never been a market town, the abbots of Torre preferring their property of Newton Abbot as a setting for a profitable market. This absence of a market was remedied by Sir L V Palk in 1820 who commissioned 'his' architect John Foulston to design a suitable building in Torwood Street.

The result was the Rotunda, an impressive circular building, with many market stalls and a considerable open space. This flourished for a while, but fell into decline as it faced competition from outside traders and street stalls. When a further attempt to open a market at a site in Fleet Street, opposite the present Post Office, failed in Parliament, and caused considerable divisions in the town,

Palk suggested a site on land he owned on the Ellacombe side of Union Street. The market building built in 1853, and restored on several occasions since, flourishes to this day.

If Sir Laurence Vaughan Palk had been a quieter individual, there is a possibility that Torquay would have developed in a very different way. He had come into his estate in 1814 at the age of 20, following the death of his father. His inheritance came saddled with debts; a great deal of Palk money had been invested in the expansion of the town and harbour, but with little in the way of return. Sir L V, as he was popularly known throughout the area, seems to have inherited his father's inability to control money. For all his good works, money seemed to fritter through his hands at an alarming rate. He had done his best for a while, improving the road towards Newton Abbot, and bringing a market to the town. The Mechanics' Institute alone is a tribute to the philanthropic side of his nature, and Palk delivered the very first lecture to an audience of working men. There were a number of other such initiatives scattered around the growing resort.

But there was another side to Sir L V Palk. He drank and gambled, toyed with the ladies of the town, and kept mistresses, all very expensive vices for a landowner already in financial distress. The prospect of bailiffs and imprisonment for debt was to hover over Palk's head for much of his life. To prevent the absolute calamity of being consigned to a debtors' gaol, Palk was forced to hand over control of his entire estate to his agents, the solicitor Mark Kennaway and solicitor and

banker William Kitson; agreeing in 1844 to a trust that would see the greater part of the income from the estate going towards the clearance of the debts, a small allowance being made available for Palk himself and his son and heir. William Kitson was forced to sell estate land near to Chapel Hill to the South Devon Railway Company to raise £4,000 to enable Palk to flee to France, where he lingered in impecunious exile.

After two years in Dieppe, Palk's wife died, and he once more succumbed to the local temptations, notably the casino and women. In 1848, he wrote to Kennaway to confess that he was 'perfectly destitute'. That same year he entered into a clandestine marriage with a French woman, borrowed money from Kitson which he never repaid, and sank deeper into debt and debauchery. By 1858, his eldest son, in despair at this squandering of the family fortunes, took steps to have his father declared insane and committed to a lunatic asylum. But this was headed off by the re-arrangement of the trusteeship, giving the Palk juniors more money, and removing many of the powers that Kitson and Kennaway had enjoyed for a decade.

When Sir L V Palk finally returned to England he was treated, by one of those quirks of English communal eccentricity, as something of a local hero. Most of the town turned up at Torre Station to greet Torquay's prodigal son, including George Pearce, the servant who had marked out the course of the road towards Newton Abbot all those years earlier, Messrs Kennaway and Kitson, and many of the tradesmen to whom Palk must have owed money at one time or another. Cheering crowds watched as the procession headed down Union Street to the Strand, where speeches were made from the balcony of the Royal Hotel. From fashionable gentry to workers and servants, they were all there cheering, suggesting that Sir L V, for all his faults, must have had a winning personality. Palk retired to his grand house under the Haldon Hills and lived in peaceful retirement with one of his daughters until his death in 1860.

THE MARKET BUILDING AND MARKET STREET 2005
T62717k (John Bainbridge)

VAUGHAN PARADE, KITSON'S HOME AND OFFICE 2005   T62701k (John Bainbridge)

The decade of Palk's exile changed the face of Torquay, almost entirely thanks to his agent William Kitson. On the wall of Kitson's old headquarters at 2 Vaughan Parade is a plaque placed by the local Civic Society. It reads: 'The home and offices of William Kitson, 1800-1883, solicitor, land agent, local authority chairman, banker and churchwarden. THE MAKER OF TORQUAY.' There is no hyperbole in that description of Kitson's contribution to the growth of the town and resort. Torquay would have been very different but for that decade of Kitson's control. His name deserves the association with Torquay, in the way that William Brewer's is associated with Torre. Kitson was held in some considerable respect, though behind his back the locals called him 'old darning needle' in respect of his appearance, or 'Penny Bun' Kitson because of his frugal eating habits.

In those few years, Kitson was everywhere and ever busy; chairing committees, bringing utilities into the town, planning roads, villas, hotels and terraces. There was no end to his involvement. Palk-owned land on the hillsides around Lincombe and Warberry was transformed into a stunningly attractive townscape of large villas surrounded by considerable gardens, reached by carefully engineered roads, most with fine views over Torbay and the rest of the town. Kitson had an awareness of the clientele that he wished to attract to Torquay. There was to be nothing cheap and nasty in this resort and in many cases the leases went into intricate detail about the quality of the buildings. Many of the villas around Torwood, Ilsham and Warberry date from this time and, despite the fact that many have been transformed into flats, hotels and guest houses, the grandeur of Kitson's overall design for the town survives.

BELGRAVE CRESCENT 1889 21460

Having complete control over Palk property allowed Kitson to deal out leases for new properties, or more rarely, sell land for houses and hotels. This was no building free-for-all. Kitson had an aesthetic eye for form and beauty and his iron hand ensured that there were no blots on the landscape. His efforts won the praise of his contemporaries, local magistrate Mr March Phillips commenting in 1874 at the end of Kitson's reign: 'To Mr Kitson's discrimination, foresight and judgement should be ascribed whatever attractions art has conferred upon the town. The hills, hitherto inaccessible, were opened up by roads which were planned by him; the symmetrical arrangement of the villas on the sloping hills were the result of his fertile ingenuity; the water works by which the town was supplied ... were made and developed under his eye; mainly through his instrumentality the town was lighted with gas; and markets, local government, drainage and other sanitary matters were entirely promoted by him. In short, Mr William Kitson had before him the building of a new town ...'

Murray's handbook of 1859 tells us that in Meadfoot 'crescents and terraces have risen like mushrooms'. The town was already reaching beyond those northern boundaries and into the neighbouring communities of Babbacombe and St Marychurch, though the coastline in that direction remained, and still remains, relatively unspoiled. The gem of that area is Hesketh Crescent, a great sweep of 15 houses above Meadfoot Beach, built in Regency style in 1849 by the Harvey brothers. The central house, latterly the Osborne Hotel, was the home of Sir Lawrence Palk. It remains, arguably, the finest example of 19th-century architecture around Torbay - as stunning and dignified as the day it was built.

Hesketh Crescent is the great joy of the mid-century building boom in Torquay, though a number of neighbouring buildings have been erected since this photograph was taken towards the end of Victoria's reign. Residents would not have had far to walk to the beautiful stretch of Meadfoot Beach just below, seen here with its bathing machines.

In 1850, William White had remarked, in his 'Directory of Devon', that 'Torre and Torquay (could) be considered as one town, comprising with its western suburbs … about 9,000 inhabitants. Such has been the increasing influx of visitors to Torquay in the last 10 years, that its number of dwellings has doubled in that period, and many wealthy families have now handsome mansions here, in which they reside continually, or during autumn and winter.' Not everyone was convinced and some older locals mourned the loss of the bare hills that once overlooked the bay. The anonymous author of 'The Handbook for Torquay' of 1854 complained that the dramatic Waldon Hill, which towers above the harbour, was by then 'disfigured by unsightly villas'.

But it was still very much a town for the upper classes and the more affluent sections of the middle class. A standard of decorum was expected and inappropriate behaviour was not tolerated. New residents and long term visitors were expected to produce 'letters of introduction' as proof of their respectability. A person's 'class' would be noted and even at this level of society doors might be barred for those deemed to be unworthy. But for a Victorian town of its size the crime rate was low and, by the standards of the time, where there was immorality it tended to be tucked away in corners, such as the prostitutes who haunted the Rock Walk at night.

Working people were not very much in evidence except as servants in the villas, staff in the hotels, and carriage drivers. But for a

TORBAY HOTEL

while the slums survived the new development regime, especially in the vicinity of George Street, Swan Street and Pimlico - the 'old and worst parts of the town' in the words of the 19th-century historian J T White. Given the central position of these areas, one suspects that eyes were sometimes averted to avoid seeing this poverty in the midst of so much prosperity.

Did you know?

Richard Burton, the great Victorian explorer, traveller and writer was born in Torquay in 1821. In 1853, disguised in pilgrim's garb, he made the journey to the forbidden cities of Mecca and Medina, and later attempted to find the source of the Nile. He is best known as the translator into English of 'The Arabian Nights' tales.

But feigned ignorance of social conditions was not always enough to prevent disaster, for it was in that quarter of Torquay that cholera broke out in 1849. In a disastrous six weeks the disease and accompanying dysentery killed 66 men, women and children, and threatened to spread to the more affluent areas. The cholera was checked only by removing the inhabitants out of their appalling environment to a temporary relocation in wooden huts at Plainmoor. The expense of wiping out the cholera in this way amounted to £1,176. 11s 6d, for 'relief given to poor persons, sanitary precautions, medical officers, house visitors and nurses'.

Two years before that, bread riots had broken out in the same part of the town following a poor harvest in 1846. Several bread shops and bakeries in Torquay were looted by the starving mob and representatives of authority were attacked in the streets. The Riot Act was read and 300 special constables sworn in to help keep order. Detachments of coastguards were shipped into Torbay on board HMS 'Vulcan' and HMS 'Adelaide' to back up the outnumbered police force. A number of arrests were made and the rising crushed.

Octavian Blewitt tells us that in the early years of the century there was even a 'Torquay Association for the Protection of Property'. It was placed under the initial management of the ubiquitous William Kitson and designed to 'aid the prosecution of persons who may be found to commit depredations on the property of the inhabitants'. In Regency and Victorian Torquay property was king, and the amount you had was the principal measure of your social standing.

Given the importance of property to many of the wealthier inhabitants of the resort, it was the fear of losing anything that prompted the creation of most of Torquay's charitable institutions. As a proportion of total wealth little charity was given, except by a minority of exceptional benefactors. In the eyes of Torquay 'society' poverty was a result of individual moral decay. The poor were poor and it was their own fault because they were simply not industrious enough. Only an implied fear of the mob kept contributions rolling in and then at an inadequate level.

Blewitt complained that 'the funds derived from the contributions of the residents are inadequate to promote the purposes of these establishments'. There was a genuine fear of social and political revolution.

Where charity was given, it was usually on the condition that the poor had to be 'improved' as well as aided. Mrs James Younge started 'The Penny Club for Clothing the Children of the Poor'. Her wealthy contributors paid a weekly penny to the fund, but the half-starved children enjoying the benefits of this enterprise had to find the same weekly sum, by which, Blewitt noted, 'it is presumed they will acquire a habit of necessary economy'. The Torquay Benevolent Society worked to the same harsh regimen in its endeavours to 'relieve the sick, the aged, and the infirm … and to stop the evils of indiscriminate charity by turning it into more useful channels'. William Kitson,

THE OLD TOLL HOUSE, TORBAY ROAD 2005 T62705k
(John Bainbridge)

This building started out as the toll house for the turnpiked Torbay Road, then served as a public convenience and now stands empty.

the Maker of Torquay, could be as hard on the poor as anyone, refusing the provision of a public wash-house for the poor on the grounds of cost.

UNION STREET 2005 T62709k (John Bainbridge)

Babbacombe is a resort in its own right, set on a spectacular cliff top hundreds of feet above its wind sheltered beach, the two linked both by a long and winding path and a cliff railway. The little town's most famous visitor was the playwright Oscar Wilde, who retreated here to write a play in 1892. He was joined for a while by his nemesis, Lord Alfred Douglas, but they had a row and Douglas returned home. At a house called 'The Glen' hard by this beach the elderly Miss Emma Keyse was found murdered in 1884. Her servant John Lee was convicted of the crime and sentenced to death. Three times the hangman tried to execute Lee in Exeter Gaol. Each time the trap door failed to open, and in the end John 'Babbacombe' Lee's sentence was commuted to life imprisonment. Some said the failure was due to divine intervention, as Lee may have been innocent, set up by a wealthy and influential Torquay gentleman who was the real murderer. A likelier explanation was that the wood of the 'drop' had swollen through exposure to damp weather. Lee was released from prison in 1907 and wrote his memoirs, becoming something of a celebrity.

BABBACOMBE BEACH 1924 76437

No homes for the working class were ever built amongst the lines of stately villas, but the situation for the poorer inhabitants of Torquay improved with the opening of Market Street in 1853. This led to the creation of an entire new section of the town around Ellacombe. By the end of the century a local writer could note that '(Ellacombe) was largely occupied with artisans and workmen's dwellings. It has been described as the "working men's town". It is entirely free from slums, and all the houses are of a superior style. It is doubtful if in any town in England, the industrial population is better housed, or enjoys more favourable conditions than in Torquay.' The credit for much of this must go to Lawrence Palk, the son of the exiled Sir L V Palk, who, recognising the scale of the problem, initiated a personal crusade in favour of better housing for the poor at affordable rents, speaking at a number of local meetings and pressing the matter when he gained a seat in Parliament.

As a resort Torquay prospered through these troublous times. Napoleon III, kinsman to that earlier visitor to Torbay and now himself an exiled Emperor of the French, came to stay in Torquay, taking a suite of apartments at the Imperial Hotel. He was greeted at the railway station by Sir Lawrence Palk, his son, and a great crowd who welcomed the Frenchman with cries of 'Vive L'Empereur'. Napoleon III was escorted by this grand procession down to his lodgings and was treated with great affection by the locals during his five-week stay, stopping to chat with many as he took his daily strolls around Torquay. The Emperor even contemplated settling in the resort and looked for a villa, but political expediency meant that he needed to be nearer to London.

Napoleon III had come to Torquay to restore his health and this was still the prime motive of a holiday in the resort through the rest of the century. The writer Max O'Rell, speaking at a public dinner towards the end of Victoria's reign, told his audience that 'the motto of the Borough of Torquay is "Health and Happiness". I am healthy because once a year I come to rest in Torquay. In the winter you have the perfect Mediterranean sight with the blue water and the purple hill.'

Others thought the resort had become a parody of itself. By the end of the 19th century, the visiting author Rudyard Kipling had come to hate the overpowering invalidity and cod-gentility of the town, making the disparaging comment, 'Torquay is such a place as I do desire to upset by dancing through it with nothing on but my spectacles. Villas, clipped hedges, fat old ladies with respirators and obese landaus. The Almighty is a discursive and frivolous trifler compared with some of 'em.'

But despite these quibbles the town had progressed in the most remarkable way from the fishing village of Napoleon's time to a modern resort on the eve of the 20th century. A Victorian visiting the Torquay of today would recognise much of the resort, though he would probably be horrified at some of the modern building intrusions. What would be stranger to him would be the patent democratisation of the 'Queen on Watering Places'. In the 20th century Torquay was to become a holiday resort for all.

Church
Chap.
B.M. 37·8
School
Devon
Rosery
M.S.
Hotel
A.L.B.
B.M. 40·1
B.M. 31·7
Reservoir
(Torquay Corporation
Water Works)
F.P.
213
Chap.
B.M. 24·1
B.M. 24·1
Tor Abbey
Chapel
Spring
Quarry
177·9
B.M. 94·1
Tor Abbey
Gateway
Hotel
B.M. 139·9
Vicarage
CHELSTON
St. Matthew's
Church
121·4
Barn
B.M. 17·8
Lanscombe
B.M. 17·2
B.M. 14·6
H.W.M.O.T.
B.M. 194·7
Recreation
Ground
Tor Abbey Sands
Lodge
RAWLYN ROAD
Grand Stand
Torquay Station
L.W.M.O.T.
F.P.
Thornhill
Brake
B.M. 171·4
Chelston
Cross
B.M. 105·2
Hotel
B.M. 30·6
Hennapyn
B.M. 66·2
40
Corbons Head
G.P. Lane
40
Hotel
21
Livermead Sands
LIVERMEAD
MARDOOMBE ROAD
L.B.
Old Paignton Road
BROAD PARK ROAD
G.P.
24·1
30
L.B.
Livermead
Cliff Hotel
B.M.
40·6
FERNFIELD
Hotel
Livermead
Cliff Hotel
93·6
Lake
Roundhill
Cottage
Round
Hill
Old Cove

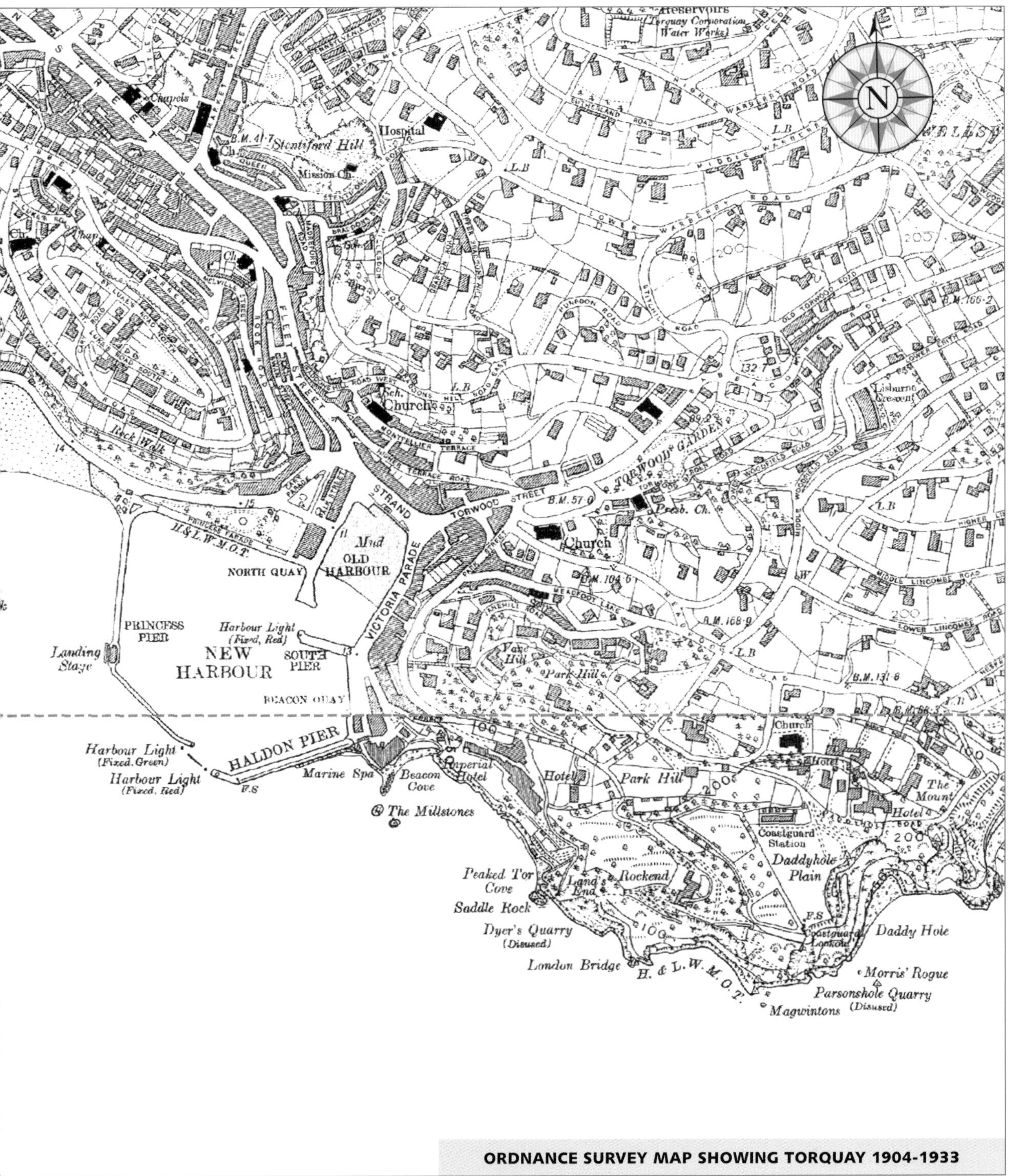
N
Reservoirs
(Torquay Corporation
Water Works)
Chapels
B.M. 41.7 Stentiford Hill
Hospital
Mission Ch.
Ch.
L.B
L.B
WELLS
Ch.
B.M. 166.2
LOWER WARBERRY ROAD
MIDDLE WARBERRY ROAD
TORWOOD ROAD
Rock Walk
132
Lisburne
Crescent
Sch.
Church
TORWOOD GARDEN
L.B
WOODFIELD ROAD
B.M. 57.0
Presb. Ch.
Strand
Torwood Street
Church
MIDDLE LINCOMBE ROAD
Mud
OLD
HARBOUR
NORTH QUAY
B.M. 104.6
B.M. 168.9
200
VICTORIA PARADE
L.B
LOWER LINCOMBE ROAD
PRINCESS
PIER
Harbour Light
(Fixed, Red)
Vane
Hill
Park Hill
L.B
B.M. 131.8
Landing
Stage
NEW
HARBOUR
SOUTH
PIER
Church
BEACON QUAY
B.M. 86
Harbour Light
(Fixed, Green)
HALDON PIER
Hotel
F.S
Harbour Light
(Fixed, Red)
Marine Spa
Beacon
Cove
Imperial
Hotel
Hotel
Park Hill
200
The
Mount
Hotel
The Millstones
Coastguard
Station
Daddyhole
Plain
200
Peaked Tor
Cove
Land's
End
Rockend
Saddle Rock
F.S
Coastguard
Lookout
Daddy Hole
Dyer's Quarry
(Disused)
London Bridge
H. & L.W.M.O.T.
Morris' Rogue
Parsonshole Quarry
(Disused)
Magwintons

BATHING OFFICE
FOR YOUR LITTER
PALM COURT

CHAPTER FOUR

Resort

PRINCESS PARADE 1920 69579

GEORGE V had been king for just a few months when he arrived in Torquay in 1910. It was an accidental visit. He had been meant to review the Fleet in Mount's Bay, in Cornwall, but a storm had put an end to this original arrangement, forcing some 230 ships of the Royal Navy to take shelter in Torbay. It was a reminder of all those earlier times of naval glory, an echo of the Navy's connection with the area during the wars with Napoleon. HMS 'Dreadnought', the country's most powerful warship, was the star attraction as it made a rush out to sea to fire its guns, and on one occasion the salvo was loosed off by King George himself.

A pioneer aviator, Mr Grahame-White took off from Torre Abbey Meadows in his biplane, to circle the ships that filled the bay almost to overflowing. As he passed overhead, some of the ships practiced training their guns on his aircraft, but were not quick enough - an ominous revelation of how later 20th-century warfare would compromise capital ships. He came safely back to earth on the Torre Abbey lawn, to great cheers from the crowds, most of who were witnessing the flight of an aeroplane for the first time. Locals and visitors hired boats to sail around the fleet, just as earlier Torquinians had set out to view Napoleon Bonaparte. It was a busy, bustling scene, culminating in King George coming ashore at the Princess Pier, to make a speech extolling the beauties of the town before catching a train back to London.

PRINCESS PIER c1940 T62386

CONCERTS

Pavilion Theatre, Torquay
Telephone 23251

BERNARD DELFONT

presents

JACK DOUGLAS

in

*"DON'T
TELL THE WIFE"*

The all-laughter farce by Sam Cree

MARINE SPA, TORQUAY

DANCING
NIGHTLY

at 8 p.m.

to the popular

IVY BENSON SHOW BAND

SPANISH BARN
Torre Abbey
*LIGHT ORCHESTRAL
CONCERTS*
by
John Allen and his Orchestra

HOLIDAY UNLIMITED ADVERTISEMENT ZZZ03795
(Author's Collection)

Festival Theatre, Paignton
Telephone 58641
By Public Demand

Robert Luff Holdings Limited
(In association with George Mitchell)
present

*A Fabulous New £60,000 Production
of the World Record Breaking*

**Black and White
Minstrel Show**

This production is entirely new to the
South-west of England

MITCHELL MINSTRELS
TV TOPPERS

and full International cast

Produced by George Inns

based on the popular B.B.C. TV Series

Nightly at 6 p.m. and 8.30 p.m.

Princess Theatre, Torquay
Telephone 27527

BERNARD DELFONT

presents

SHOWTIME

1966 FRANKIE VAUGHAN

1967 MAX BYGRAVES

1968 VAL DOONICAN
and ARTHUR ASKEY

1969 MAX BYGRAVES

1970 ANOTHER STAR
ATTRACTION

Nightly at 6 p.m. and 8.30 p.m.

Babbacombe Theatre, Torquay
Telephone 38385
EBURY PRODUCTIONS
present

AFTER EIGHT

*A vastly entertaining show with
the accent on youth and vitality*
Shows every evening

**Palace Theatre
Paignton**

A

SEASON OF FOUR PLAYS
IN REPERTOIRE

At the theatre with show appeal

ADVERTISEMENTS ZZZ03804 (Author's Colletion)

FOR RECOMMENDED

**HOLIDAY
ACCOMMODATION**

AT

TORQUAY

PAIGNTON

TEIGNMOUTH

BRIXHAM

Write, Phone or Call

HOLIDAYS UNLIMITED

**130 WINNER ST.
PAIGNTON**

Tel. 57868
(After hours 58473)

**120 UNION ST.
TORQUAY**
(Over Castle Circus P.O.)
Tel. 58139

*Also Reservations and Tickets for all Continental
Travel (Land, Air or Sea)*

ESTABLISHED 1945

**TORQUAY AND PAIGNTON NATURE-CURE
ADVERTISEMENT** ZZZ03799 (Author's Collection)

Did you know?

*During the earlier years of the 19th century,
new houses with a sea view were not so
popular. Invalids preferred residences on the
sides of the hillsides, offering shelter from the
withering south-easterly gales.*

Torquay remained a resort for the well-heeled. A holiday in the town was still beyond the resources of most working families, and there was still an emphasis on the resort being a place of recovery from illness. Indeed, the motto on its Royal Charter, granted in 1892, was *Salus et Facilitas*, 'Health and Happiness'. The town had grown considerably since William Kitson's day. In the first year of the new century, Cockington, St Marychurch and Babbacombe had been formally absorbed into Torquay, with a ruling Corporation. The First World War was to change much of this. Its outbreak had plunged the town into an initial gloom, as holidays were cancelled and hoteliers feared that they might have to put up the shutters. But, as in previous wars, a number of troops were stationed in Torquay, and it became a place of convalescence for sick and wounded soldiers.

The Princess Gardens were opened in 1894 as an accompaniment to the construction of the pier of the same name. Two hundred thousand tons of earth were dumped here to win back the land from the sea. The first thoughts for the pier was that it might just be a stone structure to give additional shelter to the harbour, but a pleasure pier for promenading and as an embarkation point for passenger ships was decided upon. Photograph 47815 also shows the Torbay Hotel, although the façade has been toned down in recent years. The hotel started life as five private houses, seen here to the right. The Harvey Brothers designed and added the further hotel unit on the left, absorbing the original homes. The Torbay Hotel now specialises in holidays by motor coach. The Princess Gardens remain a beautiful green setting for a leisurely walk, or a sit down by the always immaculate flower beds.

PRINCESS GARDENS 1901 47815

PRINCESS GARDENS 2005 T62720k (John Bainbridge)

In the war's aftermath, there was a holiday boom and a feeling that life should be enjoyed. Initially, the clientele remained relatively wealthy and there still seemed to be a feeling that Torquay was a resort for just the winter. The Borough Meteorologist complained bitterly, 'One of the most mischievous fallacies is the idea that Torquay is "frightfully hot" in the summer. Thousands are kept away from our beautiful town by this bogey. It is important to note that people in leafy Torquay do not suffer exposure to the glare of the summer sun, the trees being so abundant that there is frequent shade as well as restful scenery for the eyes.'

But for the visitors who did begin to arrive in their thousands at the town's two railway stations there was much to see and do. A guide book writer of the time noted: 'Recognising that visitors to seaside resorts seek their pleasures by or on the sea, the Corporation has acquired complete control of the harbour piers and beaches, and has provided ample and

DEVON SELF DRIVE HIRE LTD ADVERTISEMENT ZZZ03794
(Author's Collection)

ADVERTISEMENT FOR RIVER DART TRIPS ZZZ03792
(Author's Collection)

CALLARD'S CAFÉ ADVERTISEMENT
ZZZ03796 (Author's Collection)

Torquay and Paignton Nature-Cure Institute

Principal :
A. G. SPARKES, Naturopath

110 TORQUAY ROAD, PAIGNTON
Telephone : Paignton 57906

CONSULTATIONS BY APPOINTMENT ONLY

ADVERTISEMENT   ZZZ03797 (Author's Collection)

safe accommodation for those who wish to indulge in such pursuits as boating, bathing and fishing.' The Corporation's spending spree had been aided by the removal from the scene of those powerful Torquay families, the Palks, Carys and Mallocks. Henry Cary has sold Torre Abbey to the local authority in 1930 for £40,000, and the Mallocks disposed of Cockington two years later. Since then the resort has been shaped by the many and not the few. This is not to say that the needs of the sick were not met.

THE HARBOUR 2005   T62722k (John Bainbridge)

As part of the design for the resort, bathing facilities were much improved. The bar on mixed bathing had been lifted quite early in the century, this once scandalous activity now being allowed on all the Torquay beaches and on every day of the week, aided by the continued provision of bathing machines and changing tents. Rafts were moored offshore as a comfort for the less able swimmer, and concrete bathing platforms put in place along the promenades. As paid holidays became more common, working people began to enjoy the delights of Torquay, and many of William Kitson's villas were transformed into hotels and boarding houses to cater for this influx of tourists.

Older Torquay trades such as fishing, quarrying and pottery manufacture declined in importance before this newer and more profitable industry. This is not to suggest that the health benefits of the resort were ignored. Well into the 20th century, the local Medical Officer was spelling out the benefits to health of a holiday in Torquay: 'Living under such climatic conditions must be apparent to all, but it is inestimable to those who are asthmatical, or sufferers from chronic bronchitis.' But with the removal of tuberculosis as a major cause of death and infirmity as diet and housing improved, the atmosphere of the town changed from watering place to resort. The major interruption to this new found prosperity was the Second World War.

TORBAY ROAD 1920 69591

Did you know?

Until 1878 three sewers discharged into the sea, so polluting Torbay that the authorities thought it would jeopardise any chance of Torquay ever becoming a summer bathing resort of the first order. The town consulted Joseph Bazalgette, who had designed the sewerage system for London. His suggestion was a new outfall near to Hope's Nose.

On the northern side of Torquay harbour two broad slipways lead down into the water. Recent attempts to have them removed have, thankfully, been resisted, for these concrete slips are true relics of Torquay's recent history. They are the slipways built to enable American troops to embark on a fleet of ships en route to Normandy and the D-Day landings. On 3 June 1944 the American troops, who had became such a familiar sight in and around the town, disappeared on to the huge number of naval vessels moored in the harbour and anchored off the bay. The town and much of the surrounding coastline were closed to the public in those vital few days before the Normandy landings on 6 June. There was an air of mystery amongst Torquinians, a feeling that something was happening at last. People

This view of the harbour shows the D-Day landing slips two decades after they were built for the embarkation of American troops. Notice on the hilltop the crane helping to build Shirley Towers, one of the three 1960s buildings known to recent generations of Torquinians as the 'three ugly sisters'.

knew that the invasion was imminent, even the German Luftwaffe, who had attacked Torquay just a week before, dropping mines in Torbay and bombs around the harbour. D-Day was the beginning of the end of the Second World War, the process which was to allow Torquay to return to the relative normality of its existence as a seaside resort.

Just five years earlier, optimism was a rare commodity amongst the populace of Torquay. All through 1939 there was a knowledge that war was not far away. This gloom dispersed, temporarily, in July when a great flotilla of German warships, including the 'Scharnhorst' and 'Gneisenau' sailed into Torbay on a goodwill visit. The German Foreign Minister, Joachim Von Ribbentrop - a man with a fondness for Devon - had even arrived in the resort preaching a message of peace, to selected representatives of the town. It was the last such gesture. Within three months Germany was at war with Britain, and Torquay was soon to find itself in the front line.

At first, as for much of Britain during the 'Phoney War', nothing happened. During the last days of summer, and well into the autumn, visitors continued to arrive in Torquay for their holidays. There were preparations for a worst-case scenario. The ARP (Air Raid Precautions) simulated a mustard gas bomb attack on St Mark's Road. Upton School was purchased as an ARP Centre, and the Imperial Hotel had its guests thrown out at inconvenient short notice, so that it might serve as a hospital for casualties. In the event it was never used and was soon handed back to its civilian

management. These preparations seemed to hark Torquay back to those made 150 years earlier when the armies of Napoleon Bonaparte posed a similar threat to the tranquillity of Torbay. Occasionally, someone would mutter the immortal words 'You wouldn't think there was a war on, would you?,' but there always seemed to be a worrying question mark at the end of the comment, which was often met by a half-smile.

By the summer of 1940 Dunkirk had fallen, France was occupied, and Torquay was part of Britain's front line in the war against the Third Reich. Like any front line Torquay expected to come under attack before long, for this was a town under siege, in a country that expected an imminent Nazi invasion.

Within days of Anthony Eden's appeal for Local Defence Volunteers, some 600 men had come forward from the Torbay towns. As the Home Guard, these ill-equipped front line troops patrolled the long sea front and the downs and woodlands beyond on constant watch for German paratroops. Signposts were taken down, rationing imposed - causing many a Torquay garden to be dug for extra food - and gun emplacements erected at Corbyn Head and Daddyhole Plain. A line of public air raid shelters was built along the Strand, with Anderson and Morrison shelters issued for home use. Children from London, and later the

cities of the Midlands and South Wales, arrived as evacuees, most billeted in the larger villas and houses of the resort. The well-heeled citizens of Torquay found themselves

WALDON HILL AND SEA FRONT c1940 T62537

sharing their homes with the scions of the working class - what would have been an unthinkable scenario to William Kitson and his neighbours a century before. Torquay as a resort tried to 'soldier on' but access to its beaches was severely restricted with prohibiting barbed wire and land mines. Then the bombs began to fall.

On 22 April 1941, a bomb fell on The Warberries, killing two children. A fortnight later 31 high explosive bombs blitzed Forest Road and Maidencombe. Most of the raids on Torquay were not heavy bomber attacks, but 'tip and run' raids. The tactics were for fighter aircraft to come in low, below radar, over the English Channel, dropping bombs and machine gunning anyone who moved. Without the aid of radar detection there was little chance of the ARP giving much of a warning. When, on 7 June 1941, four raiders dropped bombs in the vicinity of the Torbay Hotel, the sirens didn't sound until 10 minutes after the attack. There were further raids in August and September, when the gas holder at Hollacombe was set on fire. Civilian casualties began to mount up. By the time the raids on Torbay ended in October 1944, 168 local people had been killed, a further 500 injured, with 137 houses destroyed and a further 14,000 damaged.

Torquay became notorious for its 'tip and run' raids, and a walk along the sea front could be to dice with death. One Torquinian related to me how such an expedition would mean keeping a constant eye out to sea for raiders, who might be hard to spot against the glare of the sun. Every step of the way would mean sizing up walls as places to dive behind. The playwright Sean O'Casey, then living in Totnes, afterwards remembered with dread the worry when his wife or children had to journey to Torquay for shopping or business. Local people were not in a forgiving mood. When a German fighter

was forced down on to Torre Abbey Sands in 1942 the pilot burned to death, with no one prepared to cross the barbed wire to go to his aid.

Much worse was to come. On 25 October 1942 the Palace Hotel was blitzed, leaving 37 dead. Its wartime role was as a hospital for the Royal Air Force, and many of the casualties were recuperating RAF personnel. There was particular criticism of this attack, given that a prominent red cross had been displayed on the hotel's roof, indicating its status as a hospital. The reality is that the enemy pilots may not have had time to appreciate this as they released their bomb loads and sped away, but there still remains a strong local feeling that this was a war crime. The following year, 21 German aircraft attacked the town on Sunday 30 May - an event that came to be known as the Rogation Sunday Raid. Some 330 houses were destroyed or damaged in the attack and the civilian casualties were appalling. A 1,000lb bomb was dropped on

the church in St Marychurch, just after the commencement of the Sunday School. Some 26 children were killed there, and almost as many adults in the church and elsewhere around Torquay. The fighter that dropped the fatal bomb caught the spire of the neighbouring Roman Catholic church, careering out of control to hit a house in Teignmouth Road, killing the pilot. Six out of the 21 aircraft were shot down during the raid, a loss that perhaps led to the gradual abandonment of tip and run raids.

In 1945, peace returned to Torquay with a thanksgiving service in the Pavilion, a wireless booming out Sir Winston Churchill's speech to a war-weary nation. A victory ball was held at the Imperial Hotel, but there was a deep feeling that the world had changed for ever, and that the resort would have to adapt to a very different age.

ABBEY SANDS c1940 T62406

THE DEVON TYRE SERVICE LTD.

248 TORQUAY ROAD
PAIGNTON

Telephone 82122

Stockists of all leading makes of tyres for . . .

CAR

LORRY

MOTOR-CYCLE

CYCLE

" BLUE PETER " RETREADS

"YOUNG" CAR BATTERIES

Accessories

Also at

LEMON RD., NEWTON ABBOT

Telephone 624

THE DEVON TYRE SERVICE ADVERTISEMENT ZZZ03790
(Author's Collection)

Complete House Furnishers

HOUSE AGENTS
AUCTIONEERS
VALUERS

FUNERAL DIRECTORS

WAREHOUSEMEN

16 STRAND, TORQUAY

Telephone 2288 (3 *lines*)

Established over 100 years

WILLIAMS & COX ADVERTISEMENT
ZZZ03801 (Author's Collection)

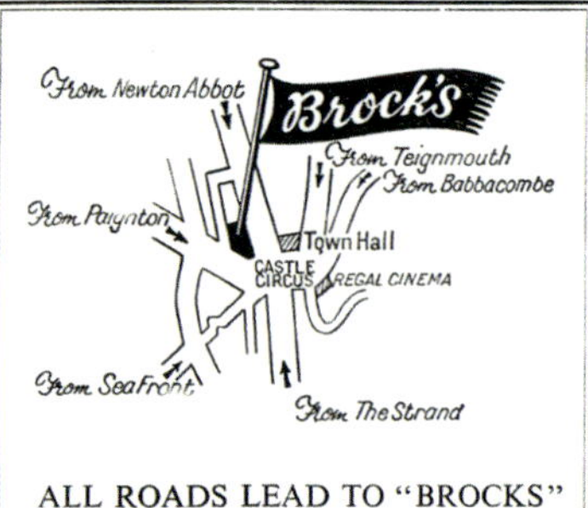

ALL ROADS LEAD TO "BROCKS"
OF CASTLE CIRCUS

THE COMPLETE
HOUSE FURNISHERS

WM. BROCK & CO. LTD.

Telephone 2703   **TORQUAY**

W M BROCK & CO ADVERTISEMENT
ZZZ03802 (Author's Collection)

ALL
BOOK LOVERS

should   visit

G. P. COVE

(Proprietors : West Country Booksellers Ltd.)

26 TORWOOD STREET
TORQUAY

Booksellers

Stationers

Newsagents

Printers

LARGE SELECTION OF LOCAL
VIEW CARDS, PICTURES, MAPS

G P COVE ADVERTISEMENT
ZZZ03803 (Author's Collection)

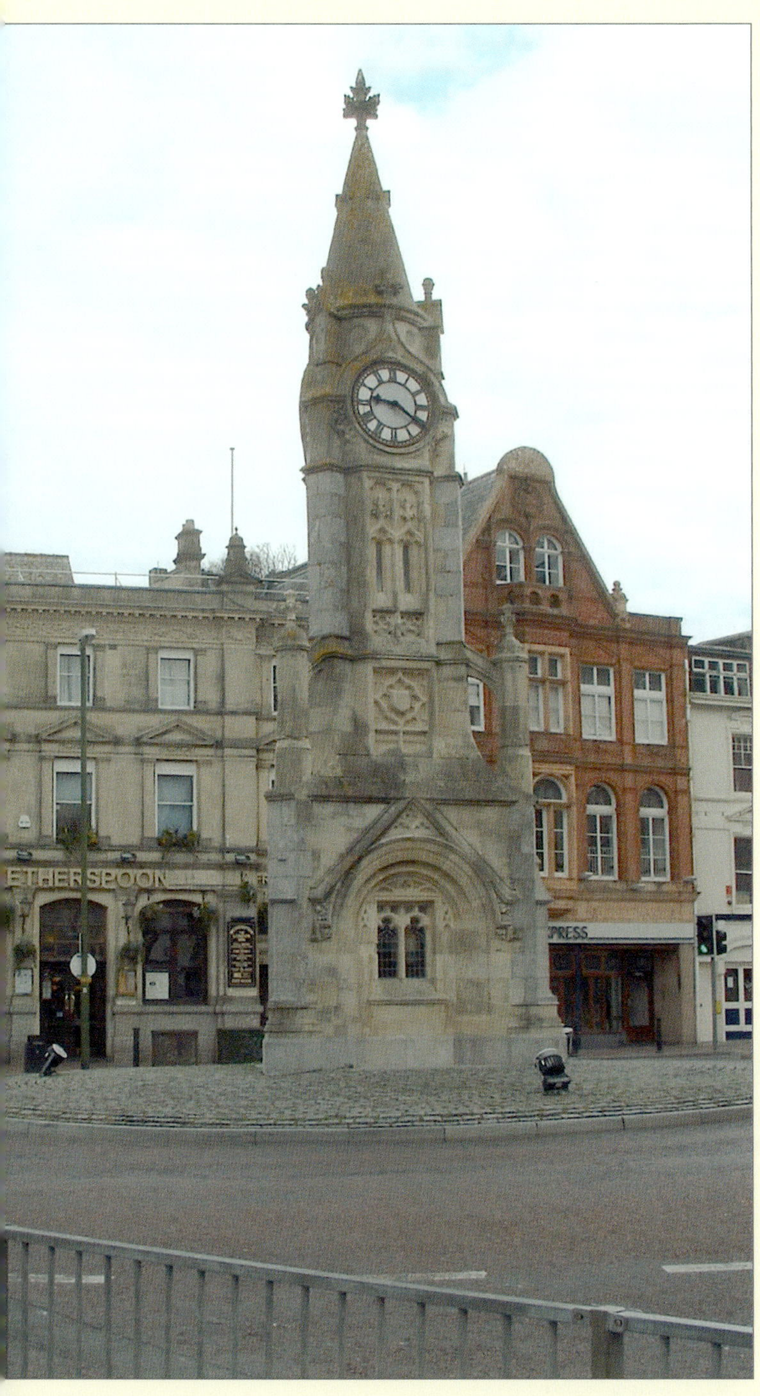

The Clock Tower on the Strand is one of the most prominent structures around Torquay harbour, although usually surrounded by very busy traffic. It was erected on this spot as a memorial to the town's Member of Parliament Richard Mallock, who died in 1900 at the age of 56. Mallock, of Cockington Court, was much appreciated in the Borough for sacrificing parts of his estate around Livermead and Chelston for necessary housing. Thankfully, he fought hard to preserve the Cockington Valley as the beautiful green space that we know today. The money for the Clock Tower was raised by public subscription.

THE CLOCK TOWER 2005
T62721k (John Bainbridge)

It is fair to say that Torquay changed much more in the latter half of the 20th century than in its earlier years. Much of the transformation came about because of the changing nature of seaside holidays. If Torquay is still partly a winter resort, then it is not in the old sense, though a fair number of people wintered for months on the shores of Torbay until recent times. Winter visits now are as brief as summer excursions to the seaside. A week, maybe two, but that is all. As we enter a new millennium, the British people who might have once spent time in Torquay have developed the habit of wintering abroad.

Cheaper foreign holidays after the 1960s led to the partial abandonment of Torquay as a tourist destination. In the first decades after the war this was not so apparent. Increased holidays with pay and, above all, wider car ownership, brought a great many new visitors to the town. There was something, indeed, of a renaissance in Torquay's fortunes. New hotels opened, both purpose-built and by way of the conversion of many of the town's original villa residences. There was considerable investment in the resort's infrastructure, such as the building of the Princess Theatre in the 1960s. The sands of Torbay were packed on golden summer days and holidaymakers thronged through the traffic packed streets of the old town.

But there were casualties, particularly in the way old buildings were demolished and new ones of poor design put in their place. Planners seemed unsympathetic to the heritage of Torquay. Many Torquinians complained about the erection of the Shirley Towers residential development above the harbour, the blocks rapidly being dubbed the 'Three Ugly Sisters'. Old dwellings, admittedly of the poorer kind, were demolished to make

way for the multi-storey car park just off Union Street in a short-sighted attempt to control Torquay's traffic problems.

One of the greatest losses of all was the demolition of the old Marine Spa in 1967, a real link with Torquay's therapeutic past having been opened just over a century earlier as the Medical Baths. It always had struggled as a health facility from its earlier days, even after the entrepreneurial

THE GRAND HOTEL 1912 64672

William Kitson had stepped in to buy it on behalf of a number of wealthy clients. But it had maintained some of its original functions well after the Second World War, offering a range of therapies to visitors and locals. It was foolishly demolished in 1967 to be replaced by Coral Island, a somewhat tacky leisure centre which struggled to make money for only a decade before putting up the shutters in 1988. For a dozen years the buildings fell into disrepair until this century when it was replaced by Living Coasts, a vast bird menagerie and aquarium, an offshoot of Paignton Zoo. Many Torquinians still mourn for the old Marine Spa and hope for a better use for this coastal site.

To cater for the conference trade, the English Riviera Centre was built alongside Torre Abbey and opened in 1987. Its design is not to everyone's taste, but it undeniably offers very fine sporting facilities, and its swimming pool is very popular. A few years before, in 1982-84, a marina for the yachts of the wealthy was built between the harbour and the Princess Pier, though, sadly, the public is denied access to its gangways.

The greatest change to the town centre, certainly the most controversial, was the construction of the Fleet Walk shopping development which started in 1988, after nearly a decade of very public wrangling. Fleet Street had been one of the triumphs of Victorian development, and its line of Victorian shops and residences was a delightful approach to the Strand and harbour. When word came out that the Borough Council intended to demolish most of the southern side of the street there was a public outcry. A 'Save Torquay Old Town' group was established, chaired by the indefatigable Mr Danny da Costa, and which was soon to enjoy the backing of much of the media and renowned architectural experts. The group favoured the renovation of the original buildings, an alternative scheme that would have allowed the public to revel in Torquay's Victorian past and Fleet Street's original shops. It was, sadly, not to be and a valuable part of the town's past was lost for ever.

This was at a time of great social depression,

Upper Union Street, together with Union Street, came into being to link the northern end of Torre with the valley of the Flete Brook, in the vicinity of what is now Castle Circus. The Flete Brook disappeared with the construction of Union Street and Fleet Street. Until well into Victorian times this area was part of the garden nurseries of the Morgan family, who are themselves remembered in the name of the roughly parallel Morgan Avenue. This approach to the town centre of Torquay will be very familiar to anyone who has studied at South Devon College which stands above Upper Union Street's junction with Newton Road. The author well remembers walking this way into the town in the 1970s whilst spending a year as a student at what was then the Torquay Technical College. Students had a very long lunch break each Tuesday which gave the author an opportunity to carry out early explorations of the town of Torquay.

with businesses failing and mass unemployment occupying people's minds. Even where there were jobs, they tended to be seasonal, leaving the once proud resort quite dead during the winter months. During this depression, which lasted through the 1980s and well into the 1990s, Torquay struggled to survive at all; unemployment threatened its tourist base and a decline in the town's traditional small industries led to local job losses and an inability to maintain the resort's infrastructure, to the detriment of its role as the 'Queen of Watering Places'. It seemed for a while that if the wartime 'tip and run' bombing raids and unkindly development had failed to devastate Torquay, then the economics of the late 20th century would do the job. The town looked shabby and run down, longstanding shops and department stores vanished, speculative building ate up some of Torquay's precious green spaces, hotels shut and stood abandoned. Only language schools and care homes seemed to thrive. For a while there was a lack of hope.

But over the past few years a turnaround has begun, which has restored some of the town's original charm. The part-pedestrianisation of Fleet Street and Union Street has helped, giving the public a chance to admire the Victorian heart of the town without falling foul of the traffic. There are pleasant places to sit for a while and Torquay is regaining its reputation as a shopping centre. There are still some areas of dereliction and a few of Torquay's older buildings are in need of restoration, but there is a feeling that the resort is on a turn for the better. Given the bombs and the planning carelessness of the 20th century, it is a miracle that so much of old Torquay has survived at all.

BEARD'S ADVERTISEMENT ZZZ03800
(Author's Collection)

THE PALLETTE ADVERTISEMENT ZZZ03798
(Author's Collection)

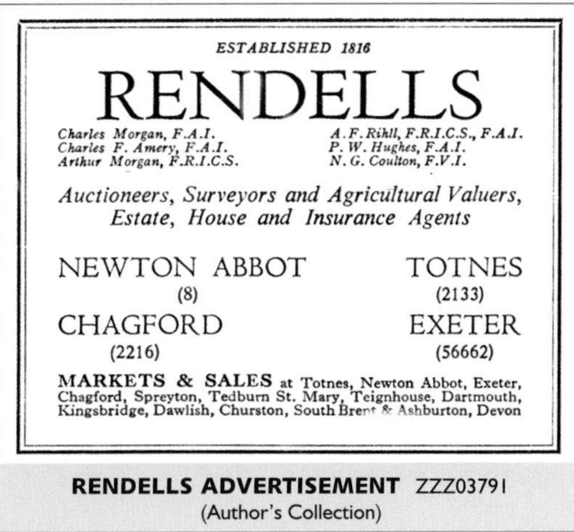

RENDELLS ADVERTISEMENT ZZZ03791
(Author's Collection)

JAYNE SILVER

CHAPTER FIVE
Torquay Now

THE OLD PARISH CHURCH of St Saviour at Torre lies concealed in what is now a suburb of the greater town of Torquay. As a survival of past times it is physically little changed, except that now it is the Greek Orthodox Church of St Andrew. Its churchyard is delightful on a spring day, with daffodils lining the pathways; a green space amidst the crammed houses that make up modern day Torre. In this quiet sanctuary is a link with Torquay's earliest times, for here is the grave of John MacEnery, (see page 15), that courageous and far-sighted early explorer of Kents Cavern. Even old Torre cannot claim the antiquity of the area's earliest inhabitants, those men and women of the Stone Age who scrabbled a living from the forests and downs of the seven hills now covered by the heart of Torquay town, known to us only by the physical evidence they left behind in their caves. It is somehow fitting that MacEnery links these two areas that play such a part in the resort's history.

Torre would be unrecognisable to its old master, William Brewer. The very rocks that gave his Norman village its name and the fields that would have been worked by his Saxon farm labourers are completely hidden under housing, shops and businesses. Yet the church survives, altered over time but a real bond with the pagan Celts who venerated the nearby spring, and the first Christians who built a place of worship above the sheltered waters of Torbay.

Downhill, adjacent to the sea, is the site of Abbot Adam's abbey. Little remains of that great foundation, but a few tumbled walls and one of the three gatehouses noticed by John Leland in the time of Henry VIII.

CENTRAL CHURCH 2005   T62711k (John Bainbridge)

Torquay has known several theatres and places of entertainment during its two centuries as a resort. The Odeon cinema in Abbey Road was originally a theatre opened by a Dr Gillow in 1879, converting to a picture house in 1934. The Public Hall attached to the new town hall in Castle Circus was designed to house 2,000 in its auditorium – used today more often for flea markets. During the First World War it was used as a makeshift hospital, where one VAD (Voluntary Aid Detachment) was the future novelist, Agatha Christie. The Princess Theatre opened in 1961 and is still a venue for popular holiday shows and touring entertainers. The more exotic Pavilion, now a shopping centre, was opened in 1912, catering for all styles of popular and classical entertainment. The Little Theatre in Babbacombe is a charming and intimate setting for plays, high above the sea on its cliff top. St Mark's Church has most recently been converted into a playhouse for the local amateur dramatic society.

PRINCESS THEATRE 1963 T62596

THE PAVILION 1920 69581

The Spanish Barn is as magnificent as ever, its great length dominating the modern parkland, once meadows leading uninterrupted down to the sea. On out-of-season days, or early in the morning before the crowds are about, it doesn't take much to imagine the desperation of the Armada captives incarcerated inside.

If you pass through the old abbey gateway, you will see the newer manor house of the Cary family. Look across to the traffic on Torbay Road and notice that the fears of Mr George Cary have come true, and you can indeed see the road from what was once his dining room. Torre Abbey is closed until 2008 for a major renovation. It will re-open as a major museum and art gallery, a fitting reminder of Torquay's considerable history.

THE ENGLISH RIVIERA CENTRE 2005   T62712k (John Bainbridge)

It is from Torbay Road that the scene would have been most unrecognisable to any but the most recent of visitors. The resort has sprawled not only across its seven hills but beyond. The Borough of Torbay, with its many suburbs, has become the third largest centre of population in Devon. Many of the green spaces between Babbacombe and Paignton have been filled in, not always very attractively, by housing. A mile beyond Torre, travelling along the road to Newton Abbot improved by Sir L V Palk, is Barton New Town, where green fields and woods have been sacrificed for homes, superstores, and a new county court building. One suspects that few residents are aware of the nearby St Michael's chapel on its secret hillside, or the fact that the back lane leading from Barton to Newton Abbot is a prehistoric ridge path.

But much of these suburbs are hidden from the sea front and walking towards the heart of Torquay, past the Rock Walk to the Strand and harbour, the eye is drawn more naturally to Torbay itself, with the fort on Berry Head guarding its entrance just as it did on those two colourful days when Napoleon Bonaparte provided such a spectacle for local sightseers.

THE MARINA 2005 T62723k (John Bainbridge)

WELLSWOOD 1890 25925

The harbour is a place to linger and much has been done to improve its surroundings in recent years. The inner harbour still caters for boatmen of modest means, unlike the vast 'marina' beyond, where some of the most expensive boats in existence are moored by the dozen, a reminder that Torquay still caters pretty well for the affluent, still refusing to altogether relinquish the title of 'Queen of Watering Places'. Nearby is a head sculpture commemorating the town's most famous daughter, Dame Agatha Christie, arguably the world's all-time bestselling author. Looking around at Vaughan Parade and the old Pavilion, we can see traces of the Edwardian Torquay where Agatha grew up, and where she came for her honeymoon and revisited often when she lived at Greenway House on the banks of the River Dart. Torbay Borough Council has instigated an excellent walk, the Agatha Christie Mile, so that fans and the curious might trace some of the scenes she knew. Whether you are an admirer or not, it is worth following, a good way to get to know interesting corners of the resort.

Agatha Christie was born Agatha Mary Miller in a now-demolished house in Barton Road in 1890. During the First World War she nursed wounded soldiers in a makeshift hospital in Torquay Town Hall, eventually working in the pharmacy, where she gained a considerable knowledge of poisons. She married Archibald Christie just before then, spending her honeymoon at the Grand Hotel. In 1926, soon after publishing 'The Murder of Roger Ackroyd' she disappeared for 11 days, before being discovered hiding in a hotel in Harrogate. Soon afterwards she divorced Archie Christie, and subsequently married the archaeologist Sir Max Mallowan. She kept a home at Greenway House on the River Dart, setting many of her famous novels and short stories in Devon locations - and giving the world those two famous literary detectives Hercule Poirot and Miss Jane Marple.

THE AGATHA CHRISTIE MEMORIAL 2005
T62708k (John Bainbridge)

THE HARBOUR c1950 T62521

Just beyond is the first view of Fleet Walk, that controversial development that led to the destruction of much of old Fleet Street. If age and familiarity have blunted its original intrusion into the Victorian landscape, one must still mourn for the original line of old shops. The entrance to the adjoining car park remains a ghastly eyesore when seen from Vaughan Parade and the western end of the Strand. If this were attended to, perhaps Fleet Walk could be liked, if never quite loved.

One of the great joys of Torquay is to sit by the harbour and watch the world go by as tourists and locals have for generations. The pavement cafés are a delight on those golden sunny days when the heat beats down and you can watch the boats come in from the sea. The area is a regular sun trap and, looking up at the hills that nestle around and provide shelter from the breeze, it is quite easy to see why this place has been dubbed

FLEET STREET 2005 T62713k (John Bainbridge)

FLEET WALK 2005 T62714k (John Bainbridge)

'the Queen of the English Riviera'. John Ruskin, the great art critic, knew a thing or two about beautiful settings and was not wrong when he compared Torquay with the great resorts of Italy. This is certainly a balmy piece of England that might hold its own in a match with Continental seaside resorts.

And who walks on the harbourside these days? Torquay's clientele has certainly changed over the years. It still attracts the affluent visitor, but democracy has prevailed and now the resort is enjoyed by all. But while visitors still come for weeks and fortnights, a number come in different ways. Torquay has become popular for coach holidays, and one of the town's old hotels is now owned by a coach company which provides accommodation as well as transport for touring. Most holidaymakers arrive by private car and no longer, as they would have done just a few decades ago, by train. Torquay Station clings on, as inconveniently distant from the town as it ever was, and Torre Station still allows passengers to embark and alight, though much of its attractive old building has been transformed into shops. However, in modern-day Torquay the car is king, only the semi-pedestrianisation of some streets keeping cars and strollers apart. Whether the two stations will survive is a matter of continuing speculation, though not enough is ever done to encourage tourists to leave their cars at home.

The Strand

These contrasting views show how the Strand has developed over the past 100 years, from the days of horse drawn carriages to our busy motor age. Photograph 69586 shows the lines and overhead wires for trams, though these were completely superseded by motor buses in 1934. The Strand is one of Torquay's busiest streets, where local people and visitors catch buses to distant parts of the resort. The Clock Tower honours Torquay's former Member of Parliament Richard Mallock, who died in 1900. The Strand boasted some of Torquay's finest department stores during the 20th century and remains a favourite place for a stroll to watch the boats in the busy harbour.

THE STRAND 1950 T62493

THE STRAND 1920 69586

THE STRAND 1906 54015

Shorter holiday breaks, weekends or a few days mid-week, attract an increasing number of tourists. Many of the small hotels that flourished from Victorian times and well into the late 20th century - those around the Abbey Road and Belgrave Road areas are good examples - are now luring in passing trade as bed and breakfast establishments, rather than expecting to be booked in advance for family holidays. Day trips are popular, both by coach and car, and Torquay has become a place to shop, with a number of fine stores luring consumers back, at last, from the neighbouring out-of-town shopping stores.

Visitors have come back, and the residents of Devon have rediscovered the delights of a day in Torquay. Shops and businesses are flourishing, the streets look brighter than they have for many years. New tourist attractions have opened and, with the restoration of Torre Abbey, there is the feeling that the Queen of Watering Places has regained her crown.

Whatever the vagaries of modern life bring upon Torquay, no one can deny the utterly beautiful setting of this town, at the northern end of its great bay. Torquay climbs around a hollow in one of the most spectacular coastlines in England, as a walk along Ilsham's Marine Drive will confirm.

MARINE DRIVE 1924 76418

Viewed from any high point the town looks delightful, especially in the early morning when it seems at its Victorian best. Napoleon Bonaparte, and those Victorian admirers, who thought it passed muster with the grandest places in Europe were right. This is a sensational location for a seaside resort.

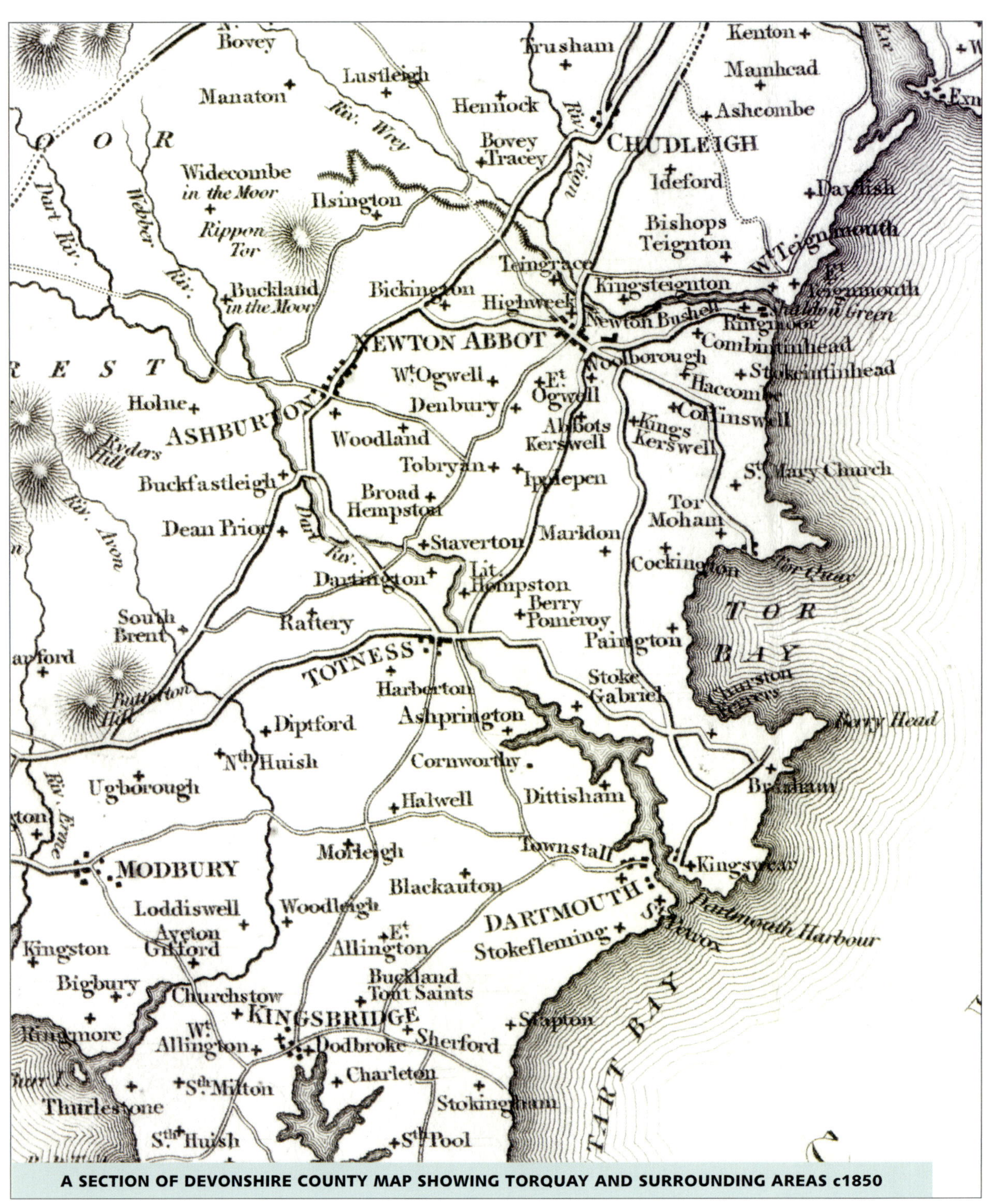

Bovey
Lustleigh
Manaton
Hennock
Trusham
Kenton
Mamhead
Ashcombe
Bovey Tracey
CHUDLEIGH
Ideford
Dawlish
OR
Widecombe in the Moor
Ilsington
Bishops Teignton
W.t Teignmouth
Rippon Tor
Part Riv.
Webber Riv.
Riv. Wrey
Riv. Teign
Kingsteignton
Teignmouth
Buckland in the Moor
Bickington
Highweek
Teigngrace
Newton Bushell
Shaldon Green
Ringmoor
Combintinhead
FOREST
Holne
NEWTON ABBOT
W.t Ogwell
Denbury
E.t Ogwell
Woolborough
Haccombe
Stokeintinhead
Ryders Hill
ASHBURTON
Woodland
Abbots Kerswell
King's Kerswell
Collinswell
Buckfastleigh
Tobryan
Ipplepen
St. Mary Church
Riv. Avon
Part Riv.
Broad Hempston
Tor Moham
Dean Prior
Marldon
Staverton
Cockington
Tor Quay
South Brent
Dartington
Raftery
Lit. Hempston
Berry Pomeroy
TOR BAY
arford
Painoton
TOTNESS
Harberton
Stoke Gabriel
Churston Ferris
Berry Head
Butterton Hill
Diptford
Ashprington
Riv. Erme
N.th Huish
Cornworthy
Dittisham
Brixham
Ugborough
Halwell
ton
Morleigh
Townstall
Kingswear
MODBURY
Blackauton
Loddiswell
Woodleigh
DARTMOUTH
Dartmouth Harbour
Kingston
Ayeton Gifford
Allington
E.t Stokefleming
Nofon
Bigbury
Buckland Tout Saints
Churchstow
Start BAY
Thurlemore
KINGSBRIDGE
Stopton
W.t Allington
Dodbroke
Sherford
S.th Milton
Charleton
Thurlestone
Stokingham
S.th Huish
S.th Pool
START BAY

A SECTION OF DEVONSHIRE COUNTY MAP SHOWING TORQUAY AND SURROUNDING AREAS c1850

BIBLIOGRAPHY

P H W Almy: Torquay and its Surroundings, 1907
John Bainbridge: Francis Frith's Around Torbay, 1999
John Bainbridge: Newton Abbot – A History and Celebration, 2004
W G Hoskins: Devon, 1966
Henry James Lethbridge: Torquay and Paignton, 2003
Murray's Handbook for Devon and Cornwall, 1859
Nikolaus Pevsner: The Buildings of England: Devon, 2001
John R Pike: Torquay, 1993
John Presland: Torquay, 1920
Percy Russell: A History of Torquay, 1960
Deryck Seymour: Torre Abbey, 1977
Tourist Guide to Torquay (Westley), 1882/84
White's Directory of Devon, 1850
The Handbook for Torquay and its Neighbourhood, 1854
J T White: The History of Torquay, 1878
Octavian Blewitt: Panorama of Torquay, 1832
Transactions of the Devonshire Association, 1862 to date

Ottakar's Bookshops

Ottakar's bookshops, the first of which opened in Brighton in 1988, can now be found in over 130 towns and cities across the United Kingdom. Expansion was gradual throughout the 1990s, but the chain has expanded rapidly in recent years, with many new shop openings and the acquisition of shops from James Thin and Hammicks.

Ottakar's has always known that a shop's local profile is as important, if not more important, than the chain's national profile, and has encouraged its staff to make their shops a part of the local community, tailoring stock to suit the area and forging links with local schools and businesses.

Local history has always been a strong area for Ottakar's, and the company has published its own award winning local history titles, based on text written by its customers, in recent years.

With a reputation for friendly, intelligent and enthusiastic booksellers, warm, inviting shops with an excellent range of books and related products, Ottakar's is now one of the UK's most popular booksellers. In 2003 and then again in 2004 it won the prestigious Best Bookselling Company of the Year Award at the British Book Awards.

Ottakar's has commissioned The Francis Frith Collection to create a series of town history books similar to this volume, as well as a range of stylish gift products, all illustrated with historical photographs.

Participating Ottakar's bookshops can be found in the following towns and cities:

Aberdeen	Douglas, Isle of Man	Kendal	St Helier
Abergavenny	Dumfries	King's Lynn	Salisbury
Aberystwyth	Dundee	Kirkcaldy	Sheffield
Andover	East Grinstead	Lancaster	Stafford
Ashford	Eastbourne	Lincoln	Staines
Ayr	Elgin	Llandudno	Stevenage
Banbury	Enfield	Loughborough	Sutton Coldfield
Barnstaple	Epsom	Lowestoft	Teddington
Basildon	Falkirk	Luton	Tenterden
Berkhamsted	Fareham	Lymington	Tiverton
Bishop's Stortford	Farnham	Maidenhead	Torquay
Boston	Folkestone	Maidstone	Trowbridge
Brentwood	Glasgow	Market Harborough	Truro
Bromley	Gloucester	Milton Keynes	Tunbridge Wells
Bury St Edmunds	Greenwich	Newport	Twickenham
Camberley	Grimsby	Newton Abbot	Walsall
Canterbury	Guildford	Norwich	Wilmslow and
Carmarthen	Harrogate	Oban	Alderley Edge
Chatham	Hastings	Ormskirk	Wells
Chelmsford	Haywards Heath	Petersfield	Weston-super-Mare
Cheltenham	Hemel Hempstead	Portsmouth	Windsor
Cirencester	High Wycombe	Poole	Witney
Coventry	Horsham	Redhill	Woking
Crawley	Huddersfield	St Albans	Worcester
Darlington	Inverness	St Andrews	Yeovil
Dorchester	Isle of Wight	St Neots	

Francis Frith
Pioneer Victorian Photographer

Francis Frith, founder of the world-famous photographic archive, was a complex and multi-talented man. A devout Quaker and a highly successful Victorian businessman, he was philosophical by nature and pioneering in outlook. By 1855 he had already established a wholesale grocery business in Liverpool, and sold it for the astonishing sum of £200,000, which is the equivalent today of over £15,000,000. Now in his thirties, and captivated by the new science of photography, Frith set out on a series of pioneering journeys up the Nile and to the Near East.

He was the first photographer to venture beyond the sixth cataract of the Nile. Africa was still the mysterious 'Dark Continent', and Stanley and Livingstone's historic meeting was a decade into the future. The conditions for picture taking confound belief. He laboured for hours in his wicker dark-room in the sweltering heat of the desert, while the volatile chemicals fizzed dangerously in their trays. Back in London he exhibited his photographs and was 'rapturously cheered' by members of the Royal Society. His reputation as a photographer was made overnight.

By the 1870s the railways had threaded their way across the country, and Bank Holidays and half-day Saturdays had been made obligatory by Act of Parliament. All of a sudden the working man and his family were able to enjoy days out, take holidays, and see a little more of the world.

With typical business acumen, Francis Frith foresaw that these new tourists would enjoy having souvenirs to commemorate their days out. For the next thirty years he travelled the country by train and by pony and trap, producing fine photographs of seaside resorts and beauty spots that were keenly bought by millions of Victorians. These prints were painstakingly pasted into family albums and pored over during the dark nights of winter, rekindling precious memories of summer excursions. Frith's studio was soon supplying retail shops all over the country, and by 1890 F Frith & Co had become the greatest specialist photographic publishing company in the world, with over 2,000 sales outlets, and pioneered the picture postcard.

Francis Frith had died in 1898 at his villa in Cannes, his great project still growing. By 1970 the archive he created contained over a third of a million pictures showing 7,000 British towns and villages.

Frith's legacy to us today is of immense significance and value, for the magnificent archive of evocative photographs he created provides a unique record of change in the cities, towns and villages throughout Britain over a century and more. Frith and his fellow studio photographers revisited locations many times down the years to update their views, compiling for us an enthralling and colourful pageant of British life and character.

We are fortunate that Frith was dedicated to recording the minutiae of everyday life. For it is this sheer wealth of visual data, the painstaking chronicle of changes in dress, transport, street layouts, buildings, housing and landscape that captivates us so much today, offering us a powerful link with the past and with the lives of our ancestors.

Computers have now made it possible for Frith's many thousands of images to be accessed almost instantly. The archive offers every one of us an opportunity to examine the places where we and our families have lived and worked down the years. Its images, depicting our shared past, are now bringing pleasure and enlightenment to millions around the world a century and more after his death. For further information visit: www.francisfrith.co.uk

FREE PRINT OF YOUR CHOICE

Mounted Print
Overall size 14 x 11 inches (355 x 280mm)

Choose any Frith photograph in this book.
Simply complete the Voucher opposite and return it with your remittance for £2.25 (to cover postage and handling) and we will print the photograph of your choice in SEPIA (size 11 x 8 inches) and supply it in a cream mount with a burgundy rule line (overall size 14 x 11 inches).
Please note: photographs with a reference number starting with a "Z" are not Frith photographs and cannot be supplied under this offer.
Offer valid for delivery to one UK address only.

PLUS: **Order additional Mounted Prints at HALF PRICE - £7.49 each** (normally £14.99)
If you would like to order more Frith prints from this book, possibly as gifts for friends and family, you can buy them at half price (with no additional postage and handling costs).

PLUS: **Have your Mounted Prints framed**
For an extra £14.95 per print you can have your mounted print(s) framed in an elegant polished wood and gilt moulding, overall size 16 x 13 inches (no additional postage and handling required).

IMPORTANT!

These special prices are only available if you use this form to order . You must use the ORIGINAL VOUCHER on this page (no copies permitted). We can only despatch to one UK address. This offer cannot be combined with any other offer.

Send completed Voucher form to:
The Francis Frith Collection, Frith's Barn, Teffont, Salisbury, Wiltshire SP3 5QP

CHOOSE A PHOTOGRAPH FROM THIS BOOK

Voucher for FREE and Reduced Price Frith Prints

Please do not photocopy this voucher. Only the original is valid, so please fill it in, cut it out and return it to us with your order.

Picture ref no	Page no	Qty	Mounted @ £7.49	Framed + £14.95	Total Cost £
		1	Free of charge*	£	£
			£7.49	£	£
			£7.49	£	£
			£7.49	£	£
			£7.49	£	£
			£7.49	£	£

Please allow 28 days for delivery. Offer available to one UK address only

* Post & handling	£2.25
Total Order Cost	£

Title of this book . . . .

I enclose a cheque/postal order for £ . . . .
made payable to 'The Francis Frith Collection'

OR please debit my Mastercard / Visa / Maestro / Amex card, details below

Card Number

Issue No (Maestro only)   Valid from (Maestro)

Expires   Signature

Name Mr/Mrs/Ms . . . .

Address . . . .

. . . .

. . . .

. . . . Postcode . . . .

Daytime Tel No . . . .

Email . . . .

ISBN: 1-84567-755-2   Valid to 31/12/08

FOR
YOUR
LITTER